Road to Emmaus

A New Model for Catechesis

Dominic F. Ashkar

Resource Publications, Inc.
San Jose, California

Editorial director: Kenneth Guentert
Managing editor: Elizabeth J. Asborno
Cover design: Kenneth Guentert
Cover photos: courtesy of St. Martin's Parish, San Jose, California

Reprint Department
Resource Publications, Inc.
160 E. Virginia Street, #290
San Jose, CA 95112-5876

Library of Congress Cataloging in Publication Data
Ashkar, Dominic F., 1936-
    Road to Emmaus : a new model for catechesis / Dominic F. Ashkar.
       p.   cm.
    Includes bibliographical references.
    ISBN 0-89390-266-7
    1. Christian education—Philosophy. 2. Catechetics—Catholic Church. 3. Bible. N.T. Luke XXIV, 13-35—Criticism, interpretation, etc. 4. Spiritual formation—Catholic Church. 5. Catholic Church—Education. I. Title.
    BV1464.A74 1993
    268—dc 20   93-17566

Printed in the United States of America.

97 96 95 94 93 | 5 4 3 2 1

To my parents,
who knew what the journey to Emmaus meant,
and
to all searching and struggling teachers

Contents

Part Two:
The Ten Emmaus Catechetical Principles

Part Three:
Teaching through Liturgy

Preface

A story is told about a little girl who was standing with her grandfather by an old-fashioned open well. They had just lowered a bucket and had drawn some water to drink.

"Grandfather," asked the little girl, "where does God live?"

The old man picked up his little granddaughter and held her over the open well. "Look down into the well," he said, "and tell me what you see."

"I see a reflection of myself," said the little girl.

"And that's where God lives," said the grandfather. "He lives in you."

This is what we see in the journey of the disciples of Emmaus. Jesus the Master *par excellence* helped the two disciples, who were young in their faith, to see in the depth of the well of their despair that God lives in them. This gave them not only happiness but enthusiasm, a word that means "God in us." "Enthusiasm" comes from the two Greek words *entheos* and *enthous*, meaning "inspired, possessed." *Entheos* has two parts, *en* ("in") and *theos* ("God").

May this little book help all of us struggling teachers to realize that the Master Teacher lives in us and that we are his reflection, his only instruments who can help others as he did to journey through the difficulties of life. May this book also help us, like the disciples of Emmaus, to find joy and enthusiasm (God in us) in being part of the Christian community, the Church.

Acknowledgments

I wish to thank my parents and my family, who taught me the meaning of the journey to Emmaus long before I learned how to read and long before I discovered it in Luke's Gospel; my teachers who directly or indirectly lived the role of the Teacher on the road to Emmaus; my many friends, bishops, priests, deacons, and seminarians who, without knowing—and more than once—made the journey to Emmaus with me; all the students, from missions to seminarians to religious education youngsters who helped me reflect again and again on the meaning of the Emmaus journey; all parishioners in the different parishes I have served here and abroad who, in spite of my weaknesses and mistakes, made the Emmaus journey a reality; my friends, priests, deacons and lay people who helped me reflect on this word through their remarks and suggestions.

I also wish to thank in a special way Chorbishop Seely Beggiani, who read a preliminary draft; Father Georges El-Khalli; and Deacon George Khoury, a lifelong teacher who took the time to read both drafts and make detailed comments; Gloria Dowaliby, also a life-long teacher who took the time to read it and make comments and suggestions; Margaret Saadi, a young graduate who also read it and made comments; the patients at the hospitals who made me see the need for developing the topic of the road to Emmaus, because in their special way they made me realize the meaning of the journey to Emmaus; and finally, Patricia Kirby, whose name should be attached to this document rather than mine, who faced my impatient temper with patience, typed and re-typed, wrote and re-wrote, searched and re-searched, and patiently continued working on the project when at times I felt like dropping it.

To all those mentioned above and those unmentioned, I say "thank you" every time I give thanks to God through the breaking of the bread, where the Lord is recognized and fills hearts with enthusiasm, meaning "God in us."

Grateful appreciation is extended for permission to quote the following copyrighted material:

Excerpts from *Les Pélerins d'Emmaus* by Soeur Jeanne d'Arc, © 1977 Les Editions du Cerf. Reprinted with permission. All rights reserved.

Scripture quotations are taken from the **New American Bible** Copyright ©1986 by the Confraternity of Christian Doctrine, 3211 Fourth Street, N.E., Washington, DC 20017-1194 and are used with permission. All rights reserved.

Part One

Evangelizing a Re-Paganized Christian World

The Emmaus Story as Told in Luke 24:13-35

Two of them that same day were making their way to a village named Emmaus seven miles distant from Jerusalem, discussing as they went all that had happened. In the course of their lively exchange, Jesus approached and began to walk with them. However, they were restrained from recognizing him.

He said to them, "What are you discussing as you go your way?" They halted, in distress, and one of them, Cleophas by name, asked him, "Are you the only resident of Jerusalem who does not know the things that went on there these past few days?" He said, "What things?"

They said, "All those that had to do with Jesus of Nazareth, a prophet powerful in the eyes of God and all the people, how our chief priest and leaders delivered him up to death and crucified him. We were hoping he was the one who would set Israel free. Besides today, the third day since those things happened, some women in our group brought us some astonishing news. They were at the tomb before dawn and failed to find his body, but returned with the tale that they had seen a vision of angels who declared that he was alive. Some of our group went to the tomb and found it to be just as the women said. But him they did not see."

Then he said to them, "What little sense you have! How slow you are to believe all that the prophets have announced! Did not the Messiah have to undergo all this so as to enter into his glory?" Beginning then with Moses and all the prophets he interpreted for them every passage of Scripture which referred to him.

By now they were near the village to which they were going and he acted as if he were going further. But they pressed him, "Stay with us. It is nearly evening. The day is practically over." So he went to stay with them.

When he had seated himself with them to eat, he took bread, pronounced the blessing, then broke the bread and began to distribute it to them. With that their eyes were open and they recognized him. Whereupon he vanished from their sight.

They said to one another, "Were not our hearts burning within us as he walked with us and explained the Scriptures to us?" They got up immediately and returned to Jerusalem where they found the eleven and the rest of their company assembled. They were greeted with, "The Lord has been raised. It is true! He has appeared to Simon." Then they recounted what had happened on the road and how they had come to know him in the breaking of the bread.

Part One

*Evangelizing a
Re-Paganized
Christian World*

The Dilemma of Catechesis

*T*he word "catechesis" comes from the Greek term *katechesis*, meaning "religious formation." This is a good term, avoiding the image of one-sided presentation in a classroom as conveyed in the related terms "religious education" or even "religious instruction." I will get into discussion of some terms later, but for now, in discussing the dilemma of catechesis, I would like to use the simple term "religious formation" to mean the enterprise of passing on the faith. Though I will also use the term "teacher" in describing the dilemma, I do not mean to limit it to those who work in a classroom, for religious formation is done in other settings as well. The fact that a classroom may come to mind in discussion of catechesis—rather than real encounter with the One who founded a community of believers—is itself part of that very dilemma.

Religion facilitates the ability of its followers to face reality, to find meaning in reality, and thereby to become more human and live life more fully. Too often people make the mistake of believing that their religious formation ends when they have completed their formal religious program, and herein lies the problem.

As a Catholic priest of the Maronite Church, I am engaged in religious formation with the young and the not-so-young, the rich and the poor, the churched and the unchurched in various settings, from the classroom to the pulpit, from the confessional to the hospitalized, and in the routine of daily pastoral counseling. In talking with others also involved in religious instruction, it's obvious that something is amiss today. Many of us have long been concerned about the failure of so much religious formation to bear fruit, such as vibrant parishes comprised of persons of all ages yearning to deepen their faith and live it. A look at Christianity in general, the Catholic Church in particular, or the various traditions which some call rites of the Catholic Church, all too often seems to indicate that fewer of the faithful—and not only the younger ones—really know their tradition, treasure it, and live it.

For religious formation programs of the minority Eastern traditions within the Catholic Church, such as the Maronite Church, the problem is compounded. Not only must teachers in religious programs within these rites deal with all the other difficulties faced by Christian communities today, but they must also try to stave off loss of their unique identity.

Discussions and conferences on religious formation abound in the Church, but I find the concern and the suggested remedies too often abstract in tone. When the words are done, the Word so often remains separate from the hearts to which he wants to come.

But when we look back at history, we can find similar concerns in every period. All that changes is the underlying illness at the moment—something that stands in the way of full acceptance and living out of the faith—and, of course, the symptoms. Thus, the task of helping the faithful grasp and live their faith meets different challenges in different ages. The challenges today will change tomorrow, just as those of the past have done. Our calling, our bond in attempting to pass on the faith—whether in the meadows of ancient Israel, in the chill candlelit cathedrals of the Middle Ages, or in the waves of telecommunication today—is simply to abide by the guidance of the Spirit, to read the signs of the times, and gear our religious formation accordingly.

Over the years, in my own attempts to pass on the faith, I have been impressed by the account of Jesus teaching his disciples on the road to Emmaus. In "meditating and cogitating" on it, as well as looking into what has been written about it, I have found some principles which have helped me immensely and which I think could help others in the same religious formation enterprise. I am not alone in drawing out principles from the catechesis Jesus gave his disciples en route. Others have also written about Emmaus as a unique setting for the one who has been called the Master Teacher, and I draw from their insights; but my point of departure is that I have consolidated their thinking and also put these principles into practice over the years—not simply studied them.

Our Need for Hearing the Good News Again

Before listing and exploring these "Emmaus Principles," I would like to set out the modern dilemma of religious formation as I see it so that we have a reason to bother setting out for Emmaus in the first place. It is, after all, a seven-mile hike from Jerusalem, and the road is downhill and rather dusty.

I think the main difference between the problem of religious formation faced by Christianity today and the one faced by the early Church is that the first Christians lived in a world which had never heard of Jesus, whereas people in most countries today—certainly in what is called "the West"—have. He and his Church have been part of our world for generations. Yet many, even many faithful, seem to need to hear the Good News all over again, as if for the first time.

As a result, Christians often take Christianity for granted. I find that, for most, Christianity is just part of the familiar landscape. The early enthusiasm and commitment have eroded. Christianity's demands may seem not just out of date but also tedious and even unwarranted in a world preoccupied with comfort, ease, and material benefits. The pagan values once overcome by Christianity are again ascendant. How did we get to this point?

Sociologists recognize that different periods in the historical development of religious movements—any social movement, really—bring changes, and that these may be anticipated. Movements go through transitional stages. Initially there is the lived experience of and with the founders—the age of the pioneers. Soon there is expansion, as the pioneers tell others what has occurred and invite them to come see for themselves. As more people respond, it is natural for order, structure, and routines to develop. Eventually, regrouping occurs as attempts are made to recapture some of the early enthusiasm and commitment and to simplify things. Finally, the movement either dies altogether or undergoes transformation into what it was earlier as well as something different. Religious instruction as well as the Church itself would seem to be in the later period of this dialectic. It needs to be transformed on its own journey.

Distanced as we are from the early historical events of Christianity, they often seem irrelevant in the Western world for contemporary life, particularly in a country which considers ancient history to be anything that happened more than one hundred years ago. We have no anchor in the past. But if we have no anchor in the past, neither do we have a link to the future for which symbols once provided. In a faith still so laden with symbols as Christianity, this situation is more difficult because the symbols once saturated with meaning now seem flattened out, becoming problematic to explain rather than providing immediately understood and dearly cherished pointers to transcendent reality. We seem to have gone from anamnesis—calling to mind as "living knowledge" what we made our own when we first came to know it—to amnesia. In such circumstances, liturgy is no link with the past, no anchor—only a barrier.

Paralleling this separation of symbol from reality is the separation of social institutions from each other. This separation is all the more true in the United States where Church and State have been purposely kept apart from the outset. Even in the so-called Christian countries, religion has increasingly been separated from the social institutions with which it was often enmeshed. As a result, religion has been separated from daily life to such a degree that when taught, it may seem merely academic to students.

When history and symbols lose their meaning and social institutions their linkage with religion, a very practical learning opportunity is removed. It becomes no longer possible to soak in religious information and witness from everyday surroundings. With no anchor in the past or pointers to the future, no wonder we lose our bearings in the present as well.

How can a close relationship with Jesus develop in a world where vibrant Christianity, once widespread and often intertwined with secular culture, is so weak that many Christians now lack even a passing understanding of their tradition? For many people, their life journeys go on with little awareness of Jesus walking alongside. They "have and have not." They may not have exactly "lost" their Christianity but they may also have never fully "had" it, either.

This contemporary situation may even affect those engaged in religious formation themselves, not just students, for they move within the same sociocultural milieu. If the Word is not alive in the heart of the teacher, how can religious formation come alive for the student?

The Teacher-Student Gap

I also find that teachers—especially those who work in the area of religious values—often make unwarranted assumptions about where their students are on the journey. We teachers often assume too easily—and incorrectly—that our students approach the course at the same point of life as ourselves, with the same desires and needs, the same readiness and eagerness to learn about their faith.

Teachers in religious classrooms are not alone in presuming student interest, of course; secular teachers often do the same. But I think the mistake is greater with the former, for what is being asked of the students is their acceptance of personal values. Why is it so difficult for us to realize that students are on the road of life at very different points from ourselves as well as from each other? Perhaps one reason is a generally limited view of the teacher as *imparter of information* rather than *developer* or *former*, certainly in the area of catechesis.

If students also differ from teachers by not always participating in religious instruction by their own free choice, inner resentment may grow, whetted ever more sharply by teachers' statements about what "we believe," what "we need" and "want to learn." Acceptance of values must be a free choice.

If those engaged in religious formation do not meet the students where they are in *their own* present journey—as Jesus did with his disciples—the students will rarely follow further, no matter how much excellent information the teachers impart. I know I am not the only teacher to discover that to succeed, we need to motivate and encourage our students to want to proceed further. But to do so, we must first win their trust, and this is my point of departure.

The information we impart must thus be more than just "head" knowledge. Students need "heart" knowledge as well, and that comes from walking with someone who has experienced the road first, then lovingly turned to help others on the road. How much more true in courses where faith is the topic, since the intellectual content is aimed to lead the student to the love of God and others. The subject matter which students most remember and put into practice is that gained from teachers who "walk their talk"—practice what they preach—in everyday life, not compartmentalizing it, as Elias expresses it:

> The journey of faith is one in which a life with
> God colors, influences, and gives deeper
> meaning to all human activities. All aspects of
> life's journey are religious. The religious person
> makes this dimension an explicit one and
> through this faith transforms all of human life
> and culture.[1]

A few years ago, a film called *Stand and Deliver* gave a powerful example of how Jaime Escalante, a high school teacher, connected in just this way with his turned-off, innercity students. He helped them grasp their need for his course to the point that they would willingly give up holidays and weekends to acquire that knowledge. Before they could reach that point, the students had to come to realize that their

---

[1] Elias, *Foundations and Practice of Adult Religious Education*, 66.

teacher deeply cared about them and was very much one of them. Only then could they allow themselves to be won over to what he had to teach.

But even such an excellent teacher pales beside the Master Teacher, who drew crowds of hearers ready to take him up at his request to become not just hearers of the word but "doers also" (Jas 1:22). Jesus met his followers, ranging from the casually interested to the fascinated disciple, right where they were, in everyday life, raising them to theological levels rarely attained in seminaries and congregations. How do we become such teachers?

The Solution: Evangelization

*T*o the problems of modern Christian—and particularly Catholic—religious formation, I think the answer is a need for basic evangelization, telling the message all over again, so that it has a stronger foundation than is often the reality today. The teaching of Jesus to the disciples on the road to Emmaus offers us a beautiful foundational model of what can be done when the telling of the message is done in such a way as to take root and create a need and desire for further growth—to prepare the way for a deeper appreciation of how liturgy can assist in carrying religious formation forward.

Evangelization, catechesis, and liturgy should help us continue to grow in our Christianity to do what we are called to do: To make the Word Incarnate, Jesus, and the kingdom of God a visibly historical reality in this world through the context of the routine of our daily life, in our place, in our time, and in our way, in every aspect of the social structure: religious, educational, cultural, economic, and political.

But what exactly are evangelization and catechesis, as well as related terms? How do they differ from each other and from what is already being done toward religious instruction? Before we start off to Emmaus to see how it might provide a model of evangelization, catechesis, and liturgy, let us take time to look at some terms that always come up in any discussion of religious formation and are all too often thrown around indiscriminately.

Definitions of Terms

Marthaler points out why it is important how a discipline is defined:

> It affects one's visions as well as one's strategies
> for religious education at the local level. It
> shapes the design of the graduate programs in
> which the professionals in the field are trained.
> It defines the relationship...to other
> disciplines—theology, liturgics, the social
> sciences, education, and so forth.[1]

Definitions of certain basic terms may seem obvious: "evangelization," "catechesis," "religious education," "Christian education," "socialization," alongside "liturgy" and "liturgical education." But these terms have posed major dilemmas, all the more in an age when even the definition of "community" is changing. If community is an ongoing process rather than an institution for which we prepare people to enter—a band of pilgrims—then it is no wonder the terms referring to approaching this community are more difficult to define.

Sometimes the first four terms are used interchangeably. They are in fact somewhat difficult to separate, as the editors

---

[1] Marthaler, "Socialization as a Model for Catechetics," 64.

of the *National Catechetical Directory*—the United States bishops' response to the Vatican II mandate to develop national and regional guidelines for catechetical enterprise—discovered. After attempting to distinguish these terms, the editors threw up their hands and stayed with the term "catechesis."

The terms bear a similarity in the learning and teaching that go on, but the context and rationale differ.

Evangelization

In the more traditional description of this term, evangelization is the announcement of the Good News to those who have not heard it before, typically but not always in pagan "missionary countries." Viewed this way, evangelization involves a somewhat different process from catechesis and religious education, for the latter two presuppose acceptance on the part of those undergoing the required period of preparation. In evangelization, it is often unclear to those sowing the seed how their efforts will take root and what to expect next in the series of rather predictable developmental stages found in catechesis and religious education.

In a study clarifying the relationship between evangelization and catechesis, Hater comments, "...evangelization is much more than teaching—it presupposes the witness of life filled with love."[2] It attracts powerfully; it makes the heart feel as if burning. The words of the message are no mere words. The Spirit has set them afire.

Catechizers build on the work of evangelizers. However, because the line between pagan and Christian countries has today become blurred, as hitherto Christian countries lapse

---

2 Hater, "Relationship Between Evangelization and Catechesis," 5.

into various degrees of neo-paganism, there can be some confusion in terms:

> Catechesis and evangelization are all but indistinguishable in practice. In the so-called post-Christian culture of Europe and North America, catechesis fails because evangelization, the initial call to conversion of life and values, has been presumed. In fact, however, family customs, national identity, schools, the calendar of holidays and holy days, and the arts, which at one time could be depended on to inculcate some knowledge of Christian and Catholic culture, have been eroded by secularism, individualism, and hedonism.[3]

Catechesis

Recent Church documents unfortunately have also contributed to the blur by using "evangelization" in two different ways, as Hater points out:[4]

1. As the *initial* proclamation of the Gospel, aiming at conversion. Catechesis thus becomes a follow-up activity. Before and after are two clearly distinct stages.

2. As *ongoing activity* of the Christian community: the initial proclamation plus all pastoral ministries that nourish it. There is no fine distinction between before

---

[3] Marthaler, "Socialization as a Model for Catechetics," 64.

[4] Hater, "Relationship Between Evangelization and Catechesis," 6. Footnote 17 identifies the Church documents that take one or the other use: 1. *General Catechetical Directory, National Catechetical Directory* and *Rite of Christian Initiation of Adults;* 2. *Evangelii Nuntiandi* and *Catechesi Tredendae.*

and after, and the role of the community is stressed.

The first use of the term "evangelization" is narrow; the second broad. Whichever use we adopt obviously colors how we use the term "catechesis," let alone how we speak of "receiving salvation."

The literal meaning of the word "catechesis," according to Warren, is "re-sounding," as in, "The earth resounded with his praise!" But, as Warren also points out, it is not a simple word to define, for it has acquired rich meanings over the centuries.[5]

Catechesis is far from being just a package of facts about God, the world, the Church, and proper commitment as a member of that Church, handed to the young person or adult convert and thus preserving a religious tradition. Personal response from the one preparing for entry into that faith tradition is also sought: belief and active participation in the Church community Thus, catechesis *develops*. It "further specifies evangelization" and is an "element" or "moment" of a whole evangelization-conversion process, as Hater describes it, pointing out how catechesis has the dual aim of firming up as well as initiating into a community[6]

Entry, however, is not or should not be the end, that is, the final point of catechesis, although too often it is just that. All too many catechumens, once accepted into the Church as full participants, leave their inquiry at the doorstep. They do not see that they still need religious formation even though they are now on the road. In fact, they do not grasp that they *are* on a road amidst a pilgrim people; they think they have arrived.

---

5 Warren, *Sourcebook for Modern Catechetics*, 16.

6 Hater, "Relationship Between Evangelization and Catechesis," 2.

The post-Vatican II imagery of the Church as a pilgrim people helps us see the need to emphasize the role of the community in catechesis. Ideally, then, catechesis should prepare for a lifelong process of community, not just entry into it.

These catechetical ideals are rarely, however, understood by the Christian community as a whole, who all too often regard catechesis—like evangelization or any of the other terms discussed in this section—as something static, something given and acquired once and for all. If they understood Neville and Westerhoff's misleadingly simple description of faith as not a noun but a verb,[7] the dynamic aspects of catechesis might well be clearer. As with "evangelization," so too with "catechesis" is there a narrow and a broad usage, which Hater draws up in this way:[8]

1. Formal or "structured" catechesis is a deliberate pastoral activity aimed at calling forth a response to God's living Word.

2. Informal catechesis is any pastoral activity at all, even if not directly or immediately aimed toward catechesis as described above. Liturgy as well as service projects and family prayer would be among these activities.

Noting that almost every pastoral ministry has a catechetical dimension, Warren points out that:

> In celebrating the paschal mystery, the liturgy, whether in baptism, eucharist, or one of the other sacraments, makes a statement about life in general and Christian life in particular. Sacramental catechesis prepares one for

---

7 Neville and Westerhoff, *Learning Through Liturgy,* 162.

8 Hater, "Religious Education and Catechesis," 3-4.

worship; mystagogy reflects on the experience
of the celebration to uncover the reality beneath
the symbols—the transcendence and presence
of God, awe and familiarity.[9]

Mystagogy denotes the catechesis of the Eastern Fathers
such as St. Cyril of Jerusalem, who unveiled the "secrets" of
the liturgy only gradually to the catechumens as they proved
themselves worthy of trust. It was not just "head knowledge"
but "heart knowledge" as well, an experiential process
geared to help the learners become more aware of Jesus
personally, all the more possible because Cyril would lead
his catechumens around the Holy City and pause to reflect
at every place where Jesus did thus and so.

Similarly for Westerhoff, catechesis is not so much the
subject matter but a process in which people learn to know,
internalize, and apply Christian revelation in daily life. Catechesis must thus be carried out within a community that
lives, learns, worships, and witnesses. In the Christian
Church, it is concerned with what it means to be Christian
together in a community and in the world, how to recall and
reconstruct tradition so it may become conscious and active
in the members individually and collectively.[10] Together,
then, as Cyril did, the catechist and his or her group journey
around the sacred places to make sense out of all that
occurred there, doing so in a living context.

The contextuality of catechesis is also noted by Campbell
when she affirms that it "cannot be separated from an ecclesial context or from sacramental and liturgical life," but
"must set out the meaning of the rites so everyone in the
community really celebrates,"[11] a clear indication of how

---

9 Warren, *Sourcebook for Modern Catechetics*, 16.

10 Westerhoff and Edwards, *Faithful Church*, 2-3.

11 Campbell, "Toward a Systematic Catechesis," 316.

liturgical ritual celebration is intertwined with the faith development process.

Although catechesis represents the strengths of one point of view, it also represents the limitations therein. While catechesis is legitimately concerned with passing on a particular tradition, it cannot contain the wide range of concerns and contexts that "religious education" does. Then too, when many of the sacred images and established ecclesial forms they present no longer shape the experience we live in the real world, when the symbols once full of meaning become empty, there can be a compounded problem for catechesis, which is the theme of an insightful dissertation by Fuchs.[12]

Despite any inherent limitations in the institutions and the symbolic systems of the religious bodies to which the catechetical content leads, however, the "lenses" that catechesis provides are a way of understanding and making meaning out of the world. If the faithful did not have them, they would be much less able to arrive at any understanding whatsoever.

Religious Education

Although "religious education" has been used to mean "catechesis," it is probably better to differentiate the two terms because catechesis need not be classroom-based. Thus, while catechesis leads directly into a religious body, religious education can be regarded as somewhat broader, bordering on, or entering into, the academic and ecumenical: learning *about* rather than accepting and lovingly responding to a call. However, some people have used the term to mean exactly that.

---

[12] Fuchs, "Task of the Religious Educator."

In the broader sense, "religious education" thus means learning about things and matters of a religious nature, not learning to adopt a particular world perspective. It might include, for instance, study of religious groups outside one's own, the writings of mystics from all religious traditions, or the formation of religious values in general.

Such a view of religious education, then, is in transcendence of the local church community, and thus it moves toward more general contemporary education. It could be viewed as a process during which a religious tradition becomes self-conscious, a process allowing an interreligious dialogue to be constructed, while one's own particular tradition is affirmed but transcended.[13]

"Religious education" in the broader meaning would not, therefore, be the thrust of evangelization-catechetical activity. In any event, "religious education" carries a "classroom imagery" that may detract from the formation process at the heart of catechesis.

Christian Education

Like "religious education," so too "Christian education" has been used in both a narrow and a broad sense. Anyone ever involved with a Christian school, particularly one of higher learning, knows something of the ongoing controversy over the term. To some, it is the study of things Christian. To others, it is a perspective on the world. To still others, it involves both. This term is not used as much in Catholic circles as "evangelization," "catechesis," or even "religious education."

---

[13] Cf. Scott, "Some Problems Raised."

Socialization

Implicit in the meanings of catechesis and religious or Christian education is that both (particularly catechesis) involve a basic process through which everyone passes, known as "socialization." This is the process of acquiring the traits of one's culture. Some might call this "enculturation." The process is really lifelong, although some emphasize the earlier period of preparation when knowledge content is mastered.

Socialization is not quite the same as the development of human mental abilities; yet it is clearly related, for humans cannot develop in social or cultural isolation.

Marthaler prefers using the more basic term "socialization" to mean the same thing as religious formation, believing that the socialization model provides a heuristic tool to understand what goes on in the religious instruction process—dialectic interaction between objective and subjective worlds—and thus a clearly defined basis on which to plan programs.[14] But he is in the minority.

The term "socialization" usually refers to a more general learning process than religious education and catechesis. It is something that religious educators at the highest levels of the Church agree we teachers need to be aware of so that we understand how human development correlates with "educability." This concern can be found throughout the landmark *General Catechetical Directory* of 1971 and the later United States national catechetical directory, *Sharing the Light of Faith*.

---

[14] Marthaler, "Socialization as a Model for Catechetics," 66.

Liturgy

The liturgy is often thought of as if it were the same thing as celebration in a particular parish or denomination. Yet liturgy should be understood as much more dynamic: the re-presentation of an earlier event that allows the faithful to re-live with Jesus the saving events of his life on earth. There is a "real presence" in the sacraments, particularly the Eucharist, the sacrament of sacraments, that allows the experiencing of the event in a way that, even though cloaked in mystery, is palpably real.

As Corbon points out in his beautiful treatise on liturgy, the word "liturgy" is derived from the Greek *leitourgía*, meaning "public service," but once the word crossed over into Christian usage its meaning broadened. Basically, however, the notion that liturgy entailed the action of the people of God (*leos*) and the element of work—or better yet, energy (*ergon*)—remained.[15]

Further, liturgy is a rite or body of rites prescribed for public celebration. In the Catholic Church, there is the added meaning that the liturgy is a re-presentation of an earlier event, a making-real-once-again, as in the events of the life of Jesus. It is part of an organized annual calendar of re-presentations in all the Eastern and Western traditions of the Catholic faith as well as certain Protestant traditions such as the Anglican Church—and the Jewish faith as well. Each year the faithful celebrate events in the same sequence, such as Christmas and Easter.

Neville and Westerhoff point out a connection between liturgy and learning:

> Liturgy and learning have been linked since the
> birth of the Christian era, but of late they have
> become estranged. Regretfully, religious

---

[15] Corbon, *Wellspring of Worship*, 191.

> educators and liturgists have gone their
> separate ways and attempts to reunite their
> various concerns have tended to confuse the
> issue and distort important distinctions between
> them. Some religious educators have made the
> serious mistake of speaking of teaching by or
> with the liturgy, thereby reducing the liturgy to
> a didactic act. To use the liturgy is to do it
> violence. Of course, we learn through the
> liturgy...[O]ur rituals shape and form us in
> fundamental ways. But our liturgies should be
> understood properly as ends and not as means.[16]

This caveat does not remove the possibility that liturgy may be the context of catechesis, if we adopt the broader meaning of catechesis discussed earlier—an ongoing, continual firming up of the initial message of evangelization, with the community as the vital context in which for it to occur.

Liturgical Education

There is a connection, of course, between liturgy and religious formation, certainly in churches which have historically incorporated ritual into their worship, such as the Catholic Church. Vatican II underlined this by emphasizing the need for connection between the various parish programs, such as education, liturgy, and service.

However, when liturgy is considered as part of a total religious formation program, it is often merely regarded as one aspect of what must be taught. Thus it becomes simply one more topic to be "covered"—for instance, to understand what liturgy is and how to participate in it, as well as perhaps to learn a little history about how it developed.

Sister M. Honor Gaffney differentiates "teaching religion through the liturgy" from teaching about liturgical subject

---

[16] Neville and Westerhoff, *Learning Through Liturgy*, 91.

matter. "Teaching religion through the liturgy," she says, "does not mean merely learning about vestments, music, ceremonies, rubrics, etc. These items are related to the liturgy, but they are not the liturgy."[17]

Rather, teaching through the liturgy incorporates liturgy into the teaching of religion so it becomes a means rather than an end. In her explanation, she cites Rev. Henry Hald:

> The aim is not to teach a subject but a living
> religion with emphasis early given to
> supernatural life and the means of growing
> therein. The procedures involve not only skilled
> classroom instruction but actual participation in
> the liturgy where supernatural life is gained
> most directly and abundantly, where Christ
> sanctifies as well as teaches. As far as is possible
> to the growing intelligence the truths of religion
> in their larger lines are drawn, living and
> appealing, from the bosom of the living Church;
> they are ordered and disposed, developed and
> brought to a niceness in the shadow of this Holy
> Mother in the classroom.[18]

This liturgical approach would extend the teaching of doctrine and the life of Christ through all aspects of the liturgy, not just the celebration of Sundays or feasts but also the liturgical year, the sacraments, liturgical prayer, and sacramentals.

At first glance, Gaffney's notion of liturgy as a means by which liturgical education is carried out seems to contrast with Neville and Westerhoff's statement that "liturgies should be understood properly as ends and not as means," because *using* liturgy would do violence to it. However, the authors hasten to show that liturgy actually does provide a way to learn as a by-product, since rituals shape and form

---

[17] Gaffney, "Development of the Liturgical Approach," 3.

[18] Hald, "Liturgical Element in Religious Instruction."

the worshipers, which is why they called their book *Learning Through Liturgy*.[19]

Then, too, the liturgy is one of the few places where the community is actually together and where there is a chance for the community to provide a catechetical context. One of the greatest challenges to integrating liturgy in a catechetical framework is to shape the community in its understanding and celebration of the liturgy as a core part of the ongoing evangelical-catechetical process.

Terms in Summary

The chart on the next page sums up, then, our various definitions of terms.

In reviewing the older and newer defintions related to religious formation, I find that the Emmaus approach seems to be particularly well-suited to the newer emphasis on the developmental process in religious formation, toward the view of fusing evangelization and catechesis. In the scriptural imagery from which it draws and from its suggested application, the Emmaus approach seems to be of great value in helping teachers prepare those with whom they work for the real journey that lies ahead.

Having differentiated terms, we can now go forward.

---

[19] Neville and Westerhoff, *Learning Through Liturgy*, 91.

Evangelization	Announcing of the Good News to those who have not heard it, but not relegated to a once-and-for-all event.
Catechesis	A process of building around a prior set of religious assumptions, necessitating an active response and typically culminating in entry to a religious group; development of personal response to the initial call.
Religious Education	Broad study of any of a variety of religious topics, thought it is often used to mean the same as "catechesis."
Christian Education	Study of "things Christian" or a Christian perspective on the world or both.
Socialization	General human developmental process through which we acquire the traits of our culture.
Liturgy	Publicly celebrated rite(s) which re-present earlier events such as those of the life of Jesus.
Liturgical Education	Teaching doctrine and the life of Jesus through the liturgy celebrated both at Mass and in related aspects such as liturgical year, sacraments, liturgical prayer, and sacramentals.

Evangelization, Catechesis, Journey, and Liturgy

Although I earlier mentioned evangelization as a solution to challenges today in preparing persons to accept and cherish the faith tradition, we cannot presuppose it has taken place among those we catechize. We may often need to provide it along with or prior to our catechetical programs for students to gain the greatest benefit.

If we take for granted that students have already been evangelized at home or church, we risk losing them altogether because they are so often not at that point in their life's journey. When they are motivated—when they know Jesus—it is then that they are ready to move on to learning more details.

Even when they do move on to the higher knowledge developed during catechesis, it must still be experiential knowledge focused on Jesus as a person. Now they are ready to meet and celebrate him in liturgy, just as on the Emmaus journey.

Instead of starting at the abstract level beyond the students and working down to their level, as so often has occurred in religious instruction in the not-too-distant past, Emmaus gives us an example of how we might move from the more concrete to the sublime. The encounter on the road to Emmaus was not learning *about* Jesus Christ, nor was it abstract theology. Emmaus was not a course in religion as something to *appreciate*, or something to *have* or *believe*. Emmaus was an encounter. It began with Jesus' approach to discouraged disciples, and it continued in several stages of his questioning, listening, and explanation—based on their needs.

It led to a liturgy, and only there did the students realize who their teacher really was, even though he was having such an intense effect upon them all during the journey. We could say that the work of Jesus culminated in the liturgy, for as soon as his disciples recognized him, he disappeared once more. From there the work of the now-mature students would begin.

Can the liturgy provide a real possibility of experiential learning? Few appreciate the many learning opportunities which exist in the liturgy to motivate and enhance faith in Christ. Through these opportunities, especially if they are all harmoniously integrated, worshipers are more prepared for what the liturgy professes to bring about—or better, *whom* it brings about.

Of course, the liturgy has always been a means of teaching. Perhaps first and foremost we think of the intellectual instructional means: scriptural readings, homily or sermon, with sequenced information and theological exposition.

The liturgy also includes affective and holistic instructional means, such as stories and metaphors used within the homily or sermon and liturgical prayers, and the rich visual symbolism found on the church windows, walls, and priestly vestments. Even though the faithful today may find it hard to penetrate the many layers of meaning of certain symbols to reveal the original realities symbolized, they remain a powerful instructional means, especially if guidance is provided to understand what they mean and to create new symbols of our own with which to express the same reality.

The liturgy, furthermore, offers concrete sensory features, such as the art and architecture of the individual church (visual); music (auditory); incense (olfactory); the Eucharist itself (taste); even the sense of touch, with the sign of peace and the holding of song or worship books or palms and candles. If kinesthetic (whole-body movement) is included with the sense of touch, there is kneeling, rising, sitting, standing, and perhaps processing.

While many liturgies may fall short of involving all the senses, the fact that they do offer these sensory features to such a high degree is the basis for cherished childhood memories cited by many stray Catholics as an important aspect of why they felt called back to the Church later. Like a diamond sparkling through its many facets, the liturgy may also shine the light to bring the faithful along the path of one or another facet to the "teachable moment" when they can encounter Christ.

The insights of the Anglican John H. Westerhoff provide some clues as to the importance of liturgy in religious instruction. He decries the neglect of ritual as lying at the roots of the failure of the Church's educational mission:

> Insofar as we have neglected our rituals, we have starved and discouraged apostleship in the world. Because we have failed to understand the important unity between our rituals and lives, we have both improperly prepared persons for meaningful participation in the faith community's ceremonial life and continued to encourage persons to participate mindlessly in rituals which often are antithetical to Christian faith. Only when we grasp the centrality of ritual for the church's life will the educational mission of the Christian church be realizable.[20]

In his aptly entitled book, *A Pilgrim People: Learning Through the Church Year*, Westerhoff points out the importance of ritual for basic human life, let alone the religious instructional enterprise, and the danger of its absence:

> We humans cannot live without ritual; our religious life is expressed collectively through symbolic narratives (sacred stories) and symbolic actions (rituals and ceremonies). Perhaps no aspect of life is more important than our ceremonial life. We humans are made for ritual, and our rituals make us. No community

---

[20] Neville and Westerhoff, *Learning Through Liturgy*, 96.

exists without a shared story and shared repetitive symbolic actions. Our understandings and our ways are invariably objectified in ceremonial observances. Faith and ritual cannot be separated....Without rituals, we lack a means for building and establishing purposeful identity; we are devoid of any significant way to sustain and transmit our understandings. Rituals, like stories, emerge from and speak to our intuitive, emotional consciousness. That explains why dance, drama, music, and visual arts are the basic means by which our rituals are enacted. And that is why poetry more than prose is the basic means by which ritual is expressed in words. When worship becomes too intellectual or wordy, it loses its depth and significance.[21]

Although some see ritual as constraining and repetitious, it may be that, as a wag once said of Christianity itself, it is not a failure, but has never been tried. If teachers of religious instruction understand and work with ritual as a route to meaning, to lifelong religious learning; if they purposefully encourage the intermixing of the human with the divine journey, harmonizing the human and divine rhythms, aware of how the human rhythm develops over the child's and the adult's span of years, it would seem that there is a promising point of departure for religious instruction.

The liturgy is the way Jesus gave his followers to meet him again and again down through the centuries, no matter how distanced from his days on earth. Only through the liturgy did the apostles recognize their friend and Lord. While we can meet him personally outside the liturgy, it is there where he has chosen to be present in such a special way—to show himself in the light. In this regard, it might be helpful to recall that the definition of "to educate" is, literally,

---

[21] Westerhoff, *Pilgrim People*, 7-8.

"to lead out [from darkness]." In describing the light, Christ once equated it with himself: "I am the light of the world" (Jn 8:12). He did not say that he *had* the light, but that he *is* the light, as prayers attest: "In your light may we see the light, Fountain of Light."[22]

In addition to providing light to follow him, Christ said, "I am the Way." This means that he is also the journey! The Catholic liturgy, in which he becomes real on the altar, has always provided a direct way to the Way. We've already noted how it can be a learning opportunity. But that experiential opportunity is not restricted to the church building; it must be taken back outside. The faithful carry on liturgical life by following the Church year, as it passes sequentially in the three concentric cycles of yearly, seasonal, and weekly celebration, from one event to another of the life of Jesus. Following Jesus is a process of gaining more light in order to continue on the road.

The Relevance of Emmaus

My aim is to address the difficulty that the particular needs—the signs!—of our times call for in catechesis so we can meet the students on their own road and give them a chance to experience Christ personally. A model is always helpful to guide teachers in helping students acquire faith (light) and experience Christ personally (journey). I have found that model in the events on the road to Emmaus. Moule explains the imagery of this account:

> In the first place, the story is a life-lesson. No metaphor for human life, considered in its activities and its conduct, is more familiar in Scripture than "the walk." Who does not recall

---

[22] "Hymn of Light," Maronite Syriac liturgy.

> the Psalmist's words, "I will walk before the
> Lord in the land of the living," [and] "I will
> walk at liberty, for I seek Thy precepts"? And
> the Prophet's, "Let us walk in the light of the
> Lord"? And the Apostle's, "We walk by faith,
> not by sight," [and] "not after the flesh, but after
> the Spirit"? The two travelers, pacing that track
> beneath the slowly westering sun, are a parable
> for all time of the Christian Pilgrim on his
> Progress to the Celestial City.[23]

A catechetical approach based on following Christ in the footsteps of the apostles at Emmaus would be dynamic indeed, for it would take into consideration the fact that he, the unchangeable, has changeable followers, never the same from moment to moment, from year to year, or from one stage of life to another. In Emmaus is a practical as well as sublime model for teachers on how to address the divine and the human dimensions in their courses so that their students might one day exclaim with Paul, "I live no longer but Christ lives in me" (Gal 2:20). This is, after all, the goal of religious formation.

The simplicity and power of Luke's story of Emmaus appeals to me because it portrays the two disciples as not only met by a concerned Jesus on the road but also as full of anguish and despair, turning their back on all they had hoped for, unable to recognize him until the liturgical event at their journey's end. As a priest, I was interested in the importance of the liturgical breaking of bread as a means of revealing the hidden Jesus.

I find particularly appealing for catechists the fact that in the Emmaus story, Jesus does not wait for his apostles but goes to meet them on the road exactly at the point where they were in their faith journey, taking all aspects of their psychosocial development into consideration. I also find appealing how his patience and love won over, dispelling the

---

[23] Moule, *Emmaus*, 57-58.

discouragement and even despair of the journeying apostles, when finally at the eucharistic meal at journey's end, "their eyes were open." In Jesus of Emmaus, there seems to be an often-overlooked model of the highest form of catechesis and one that therefore needs to be studied and imitated carefully. I find it hard to understand why this model has not been more widely discussed and analyzed within the Church, but that is what I will do in this book.

I am also attracted by the Emmaus imagery of journey within catechesis, linked as it is to human development. The imagery of life as a journey is fairly common within and outside the Church, but it could be joined with the new insights to be gained from the overall Emmaus catechetical model. It helps make the faith-acquisition process more dynamic, as Elias does when he subsumes faith development as a dimension of the journey of the human developmental process. Faith development includes but transcends psychosocial development—physical, intellectual, emotional, moral, and social capacities—involving the further dimension of the holy and transcendent in all these human areas of growth, as Elias, quoted earlier, puts so well:

> The journey of faith is one in which a life with
> God colors, influences, and gives deeper
> meaning to all human activities. All aspects of
> life's journey are religious. The religious person
> makes this dimension an explicit one and
> through this faith transforms all of human life
> and culture.[24]

I also find particularly interesting the implications of Emmaus for the celebration of earthly liturgy as a part of the unending "heavenly liturgy" that began at the resurrection. According to this insight, every liturgy—even half-hearted ones—take the faithful into the presence of the Father, Son,

---

[24] Elias, *Foundations and Practice of Adult Religious Education*, 68.

and Holy Spirit, where Mary the Blessed Mother, all the angels and saints (including the non-canonized) continually worship "in spirit and in truth." This notion of the ongoing linkage of worshipers at the earthly and heavenly liturgy was long accepted by the Church but not loudly proclaimed in the modern age, although the new *Catechism for the Catholic Church* has refocused on it.

Corbon describes this "heavenly liturgy" as "the fontal liturgy in which the life-giving humanity of the incarnate Word joins with the Father to send forth the river of life."[25] What fuller religious instruction could there be than participation in earthly liturgy that takes us into direct contact with the heavenly liturgy?

If liturgy is truly a way to *know*—in the Biblical sense of knowing from direct personal relationship—and a way to enter into the heavenly mysteries beyond the scope of mere intellectual study, then it should be a way to move the learner from mere factual knowledge to knowledge that is direct, personal, intimate, prized and cherished. Allowing experiential reliving of the life of Jesus as it does, the liturgy should be a superb means by which to not only follow but also travel and thus experience Jesus, the Way. At its core, that is exactly what every liturgy already offers, for as symbol, liturgy by definition must offer what it symbolizes. However, liturgy and liturgical education could be far more like a field trip— "going there"—in which information can really come alive.

The Eucharist at Emmaus seems to provide an excellent model of how liturgy may be an end in itself, yet also, because of that resplendent position, a means as well. In addition to serving as a model for religious educators, it could lend itself to revitalization of the liturgy along the guidelines of Vatican II.

Finally, the Emmaus catechetical model might be useful not only for catechists but also for the faithful themselves, in

---

[25] Corbon, *Wellspring of Worship*, 37.

the same way that helping learners understand something of the general and developmental learning process can be a powerful addition to the course of study. Perhaps it would help them better appreciate how Jesus acts as Teacher along life's road, walking as he did on the Emmaus road with the apostles, turning back to give a word of encouragement when he notices a lag in the pace and the heart—and leading toward the breaking of the bread.

Writers on the Emmaus Events

Today's consensus about Luke is that his forms, story atmosphere, structure, and strategy may be mainly catechetical for the new generation of Christians for whom he wrote, not strictly factual.[26] So there are those who say the Emmaus events never really happened as presented, except in Luke's imaginative literary construction. As for myself, I believe the events are historical, but it does not really matter. The story is inspired as is everything in God's Word.

Without getting into detailed theological discussion, let us pause for a look at Luke as the source of the story. It will help explain the reasons why his account of Emmaus and other events has been questioned as to historicity.

Doohan, in summing up centuries of reflection on Luke, notes that the Gospel writer is one of the earliest great pastoral and spiritual theologians. Writing at a somewhat later date than the first evangelists, he was particularly concerned with issues facing the Church of his day. Unlike the other evangelists, he came from and wrote for a Gentile world.

> Luke is no mere compiler, chronicler, or secretary. He is unquestionably one of the greatest figures of New Testament times,

---

[26] Doohan, *Luke*, 33.

placing his talents of culture and education at
the service of a reincarnation of the gospel
message. The major quality of Luke is his sense
of responsibility for the message of Christ; he is
a steward of the tradition. This does not lead
him to slavishly repeat that tradition; rather, he
is an artist, a genuine author who tells the
message of Jesus for people Jesus never knew.
He dares to discover new religious concepts to
describe Jesus....[27]

The events of Emmaus, in which we hope to find an
approach for today's catechists, are presented by only one of
the evangelists, Luke. As a professional—traditionally
thought to be a doctor—he was used to looking at small
details as symptoms and thus as parts of a larger picture. The
following paragraph summarizes Luke's account.

The disciples left Jerusalem, discouraged, heading toward Emmaus. Jesus took the first steps toward them on the
road. Although they did not recognize him, he walked along
with them. Addressing their needs, he helped them interpret
their experience, then waited to see what they would do with
what he had given them. Their hearts burning, they urged
him to stay for a meal, which ended as a liturgy, and finally
they recognized him. He disappeared and they returned to
Jerusalem to share the good news.

It is strange that while the process Jesus used has been
extensively analyzed over the centuries by those interested
in the secret of his success as a teacher, there seems to be little
written about the Emmaus story in particular, although it
may have been the subject of many unrecorded sermons.

Several years ago I was impressed by the treatise of Henri
Buisson, S.J., who traced eight pedagogical techniques that
Jesus engaged in the catechesis on the Emmaus road. Buisson
suggested that catechists should adopt those techniques as

---

[27] Doohan, *Luke*, 12.

their own.[28] His article pointed to the liturgy as the culmination of the pedagogy, but he did not directly suggest that liturgy become a means of religious formation. I adapted Buisson's ideas and added some of my own for a conference session of Maronite catechists, whose feedback was quite enthusiastic. It was then that I thought about the possibility of developing the theme further.

Later, I found a handful of other writers who had analyzed the Emmaus events in some depth, such as Joseph A. Fitzmyer, S.J., Bernard Gillièron, Right Rev. Handley Carr Glyn Moule, Soeur Jeanne d'Arc, and Stuart McAlpine. They searched the Emmaus account deeply for what it might offer beyond the mere historical details. I was particularly interested that Soeur Jeanne d'Arc directly linked Emmaus and catechetical teaching through the liturgy, as I will note later.

However little or much the Emmaus story has been analyzed in the literature, it is one of the best-known and best-loved passages in Scripture; it is a fascinating story, upbeat, beautifully crafted, deeply human, and literarily well done.

But Luke's purpose appears to be catechesis even more than just a retelling of the events. Kevane believes so: "It was He who gave the first catechism lesson to His two disconsolate followers on the road out of Jerusalem toward Emmaus, on the first Easter Sunday."[29]

As Soeur Jeanne d'Arc draws out in the diagram on the next page, there is an intricate parallelism between the earlier and later events of the story. Could something so well-constructed occur merely by pure chance? It is unlikely.

---

[28] Buisson, "Le Christ," 67-72.

[29] Kevane, *Creed and Catechetics*, 39-40.

The Great Encasement: Luke's Construction of the Story of Emmaus[30]

A They **told**

  B **Peter**, however, ran to the tomb

    C They **see** the linen wrappings

      D Two of them went on the road **from Jerusalem**

        E Discussing **together**

          F **Jesus approached**

            G But **they** were constrained from **recognizing** him

In Distress

              H They **halted**

                I Dialogue

                  J **The (things) that had to do with Jesus**

                    K "O foolish ones and slow to believe!" **The Prophets**

                      L "Did not the Messiah have to suffer to enter his glory?"

                  K' Beginning with Moses and **all the prophets**

                J' He interpreted **every passage which referred to him**

Hearts Burning

              I' Dialogue

            H' He **went in to stay with them**

            G' **Their eyes** were opened and they **recognized** him

          F' **He** vanished from their sight

        E' They discussed the events **with each other**

      D' They returned **to Jerusalem**

    C' **He appeared**

  B' To **Simon**

A' They **recounted**

---

[30] Jeanne d'Arc, *Les Pélerins d'Emmaüs*, following page 211.

Doohan notes, as Soeur Jeanne d'Arc shows so well in her diagram, that Luke paired the events in his story. This pairing is common in Luke; Doohan reports it as the "law of two." Luke tends to balance his narratives by placing two stories side by side or else introduce them with the same question, key words, or content so as to help the reader grasp their complementarity.[31]

Guitton names the Emmaus account as the one Gospel story above all others that he would preserve from extinction because it is a tender human mystery and also a progressive unveiling of that mystery. Yet the story remains clouded by mystery, as he admits:

> [T]here exists a secret relationship between this scene of Emmaus and the art of painting.
> What does the painter of light set out to do when he wishes to translate through it the mystery of being itself, if not to make the Obscure penetrate the Clear and the Clear, the Obscure? By intermixing colors, the painter wishes to give objects this profound dimension, open toward what is inside, which forms the creature's beauty...[32]

The clarity and the mystery attest to the simple Emmaus story as built on different layers of meaning, which Joseph A. Fitzmyer, S.J., and Soeur Jeanne d'Arc, approaching Emmaus independently, have unearthed. They come up with various layers, which I will collapse into three: Emmaus as factual account, as catechesis, and as eucharistic model.

---

[31] Doohan, *Luke*, 35.

[32] Guitton, "Les Disciples d'Emmaus," 160.

Emmaus As Factual Account

The Emmaus events comprise a story that took place in a particular geographical location. Soeur Jeanne d'Arc points out that the story bears the stamp of reality:

> Jesus does not float between earth and Heaven. Nothing could be less mythical or grandiose— or more discreet; no sublime inquiry; no apocalyptic note: simplicity itself. Clearly the tone is of an account wishing to give us testimony, testimony concerning a lived experience.[33]

Luke builds suspense as we enter into the meeting of the stranger and disciples, their conversation, their meal, and the disciples' return to Jerusalem. The account is one of the best constructed of all Scriptural texts in its complexity and interwovenness, yet it is simple and direct.

Emmaus As Catechesis

There are several things to learn on the road to Emmaus. In the first place, the disciples learn gradually the stranger's identity. However, this is not the entire learning content. The disciples' earlier understanding of Jesus was inaccurate, and he needed to straighten out their thinking.

Perhaps one of Luke's main reasons for focusing so much on this story was to try to address the dilemma of the early Christians in their increasing bewilderment about where Jesus was, in light of their expectations of his forthcoming return. The Emmaus account could thus serve as a metaphor, a model for the entire Christian faith adventure, as Gillièron suggests.

The story shares with several other Gospel accounts a travel imagery that may be related to that of human devel-

---

[33] Jeanne d'Arc, *Les Pélerins d'Emmaüs*, 95.

opment and the process of education itself: seeking, moving on, encountering difficulties, continuing once again:

> The rough, rocky road almost becomes that which Acts simply calls "The Way": those who walk toward God serving and praying to Him. We have already pointed out the importance of pilgrimage in Luke. More than any other, he has this sense of journeying—which is why the travel theme has such an emphasis in his writing: this great "going up toward Jerusalem," so charged with symbols, which fills half his Gospel (9,51 to 18,4)...
>
> Here, the trip is described from the disciples' vantage point: their so often misunderstood encounter with Jesus. They could walk blind at His side for such a long time on that road without recognizing Him. It was only after a shock they discovered that He was there, that He accompanies us step by step along our dark road. This is a teaching on the life of faith, on the mysterious presence of the Lord Who remains with us on all our roads, in all our despair and obscurity.
>
> There is a sense of progress on the journey, with its characteristic stages...the slow, dry, preparatory walk, where it seems that nothing is clear; then the light, brighter and brighter, which warms our hearts; then the presence, the experience of the presence, the ineffable moment which irradiates our whole life...[34]

Emmaus As Eucharistic Model

As liturgical ambience, the Emmaus story is presented as the breaking of the bread to evoke in its hearers the linkage with and teaching on the Eucharist. We who worship at

---

[34] Jeanne d'Arc, *Les Pélerins d'Emmaüs*, 98-99.

liturgy have a charming snapshot of that earliest of liturgies, and are brought into intimacy with the Celebrant and guests. When we think about it, all the earlier events on the road parallel the preliminary parts of the liturgy: moving from the hearing of the Word into the sharing of the meal. Luke gives a whole catechesis on the liturgical mystery, as Soeur Jeanne d'Arc notes:

> He makes Himself the host of men; He gives them, and continues to give a supernatural bread. In this contact with Him, in a special way, [their] faith knows Him. The two men whose eyes were closed recognized Jesus precisely in the liturgical context where Christians know Christ....Luke wishes to teach us that Christians have the same encounter in the Eucharist.
>
> He thinks of those assembled in the early Church, of those meals where brothers came together for the breaking of bread. Jesus was there as a stranger that no one recognizes at first, but in breaking the bread and consuming the Eucharist, eyes open, and by faith the faithful discover that He is there.[35]

And thus the mention at the beginning of the narrative on "the same day" (v. 13) is strongly liturgical. It was "the first day of the week," the day after the Sabbath. Exegetes have remarked that for Luke, who has woven together so many events in a single day, it would have taken a day of forty-eight hours! But has this day not become the Lord's Day, the dies dominica, when, every Sunday, we celebrate at the same time his Pasch, his death, his resurrection, his glorification, events with no measure in common with time? This mention of "the same day" clearly shows the intent of the account which we are trying to highlight: It is not mea-

---

[35] Jeanne d'Arc, *Les Pélerins d'Emmaüs*, 99-100.

sured in clock time, but it has already comprised the liturgical condensation of time of the Christian Sunday.

We find an implication at the Emmaus Eucharist that the
manner in which Jesus will be present to the disciples after
his ascension is not in a visible form but in the breaking of
the bread. In terms of role, here at the liturgy Jesus has
changed to host rather than teacher. Everyone is welcome. If
we do not see him directly, we can see him reflected in the
other guests.

While we can now appreciate what the Emmaus events
show of how Jesus teaches, what can they offer today's
catechists by way of specific approach?

The Emmaus Catechetical Principles

For those involved in religious formation, Buisson finds
eight principles embedded in the account of Jesus and the
disciples going to Emmaus:

> Jesus approached the disciples in person. He
> walked along with them. He said to them,
> "What are you discussing as you go your way?"
> Then He said to them, "O foolish ones, slow to
> believe all that the prophets foretold!" He made
> as if to go further. Once at the table, He took
> bread, blessed it, broke it, and gave it to them.
> Their eyes were opened; they recognized Him.
> They spoke with each other. They got up
> immediately and returned to Jerusalem, where
> they found the Eleven assembled.[36]

Yet there is more to Emmaus than the recorded events.
The teacher on the road was someone who knew himself—
what his identity and mission were. In that knowledge, he

---

[36] Buisson, "Le Christ," 67-72.

could reach out to others successfully. The Emmaus events could not have happened had he not known who he was and what his mission was about. So to Buisson's eight principles, I would like to add two more, and thus my list becomes:

1. Jesus knew himself—what his identity was, who he was.

2. Jesus knew his mission, what he was about.

3. Jesus approached the disciples in person.

4. Jesus walked along with them.

5. He said to them, "What are you discussing as you go your way?"

6. Then he said to them, "O foolish [dear witless] ones, slow to believe all that the prophets foretold!"

7. He made as if to go further.

8. Once at the table, he took bread, blessed it, broke it, and gave it to them, whereupon their eyes were opened and they recognized him.

9. They spoke with each other.

10. They got up immediately and returned to Jerusalem.

What Jesus did on the road follows the best insights from human development and educability. His catechetical technique was holistic and experiential, engaging the whole person. It was intellectual as well as affective. It also proceeded in a sequence, starting where the learners were, with their own particular set of needs. In fact, the journey on the road mirrors the sequential process of learning itself.

The Emmaus road can teach us something else too. Like Jesus, we teachers need to have walked the road first. We in religious instruction all too often have not done so. Without having taken the trip ourselves, we cannot teach in such a way that the students sense their teachers know the message from personal experience. We ourselves must have met Jesus, like the disciples on the road, and let him create a burning heart in us. We need to have completed our own walk with him on that road to Emmaus and back before we try to instruct, or we risk teaching in our own name rather than his. Like Jesus', our message must flow from our very being, from our entire life. Only then can we take the first step toward our students.

Yet we don't have to be expert theologians like Jesus, nor do our students need to be in despair like the disciples; Emmaus need not be carried that far. All that the story tells us, all that is required, is that we, like Jesus, keep our students at the point of departure, because as far as they are concerned the most important thing in learning is the teacher and only secondarily the message.

Acceptance of the teacher is all the more important in a subject where values as well as knowledge are imparted, as is the case with religion. If students are to accept the values and thus the message fully, they need to believe that the teacher has their best interests at heart. The mistake that we religious teachers often make in presenting the Christian message is to put the message first, even as important a message as religion. At Emmaus, Jesus is clearly a model of the patient teacher, journeying slowly with his students at their pace, gradually bringing the disciples to believe in the mystery of the resurrection. He did not mind slowness or denseness on the part of his learners as long as they were still traveling, still seeking.

The disciples accepted the words of the stranger because they accepted him—more remarkable because initially they thought him a particularly dense stranger at that! This aspect of Emmaus also tells us that we need not worry that we have little time to get our message across. Jesus worked no miracles on the road. He did not have the latest educational equipment at hand. He had only himself.

Emmaus is not the only Gospel episode where God's assistance is described in terms of a gradual movement toward faith. We have the account of the Samaritan woman and the blind man in St. John's Gospel. Sometimes these stories even take place on a road, as in the story of the Good Samaritan on the road to Jericho and of the eunuch who sought the meaning of the scriptural passage he was reading while traveling the road from Gaza. Luke also tells these "road stories" in addition to the Emmaus account. As Soeur Jeanne d'Arc points out, the center of each of these three accounts in Luke is Jerusalem:

> The accounts spread out in all directions: to Jericho, directly east; to Gaza, towards the south; and Emmaus, somewhat toward the northwest. Coming from Jerusalem, one could only "descend"....Emmaus mentions "to go on the road," stressing its aspect of journey...this word comes up four times and leads to an important catechetical point.
>
> In each account the travelers are in a state of deprivation or distress. In the Good Samaritan parable, the wounded man has been stripped, almost dead. The Emmaus pilgrims are deprived of the great messianic hope they had placed with Jesus of Nazareth. The eunuch cannot understand what he is reading.
>
> In each story something is used: water, bread, wine and oil. There is a departure and a return.
>
> The [Emmaus] parable offers us above all contemplation on the mystery of Christ come to save us. It resembles in one fell swoop the whole design of God; it contains the entire Bible from Genesis to Revelation, from the wounding

of man to the return of Christ. It comprises the messianic revelation par excellence, the revealing of the mission of the Son.

Seven miles separated Jerusalem from Emmaus. A gradual walking pace is about four miles an hour, not counting rests. So Christ had only a few hours on the road to help the two disciples pass through the steps of the journey from sadness and discouragement to the joy of the Resurrection. This moment had been well prepared for, because of the intensity created by the Passion events and because the disciples had sought long and hard. That is one reason why the lesson could go as quickly as it did.[37]

By contrast, we who are involved in religious formation may need to journey for a long time with our students, particularly young people, before the contact is established and their consciousness is opened. Respect for the process and the need for journey must be uppermost in our minds so that we avoid going too fast or too slowly.

This understanding should give courage to catechists, for if, as Buisson says, at the end of the road only one of those we are preparing says to the Lord, "Stay with us," it is worth the painful effort. It would then not be in vain because this one student would tell his companions how his heart was burning throughout the journey. In the wake of such a witness, the spirit of the whole group may gradually change.[38]

Though the Emmaus pedagogy is a unity, each piece fitting in with the others, and although all ten steps are important, three seem especially critical for those of us in the religious formation enterprise:

---

[37] Jeanne d'Arc, *Les Pélerins d'Emmaüs*, 118-119.

[38] Buisson, "Le Christ," 72.

1. The teacher meets the students at the stage of their journey on the road.

2. The teacher keeps in mind that the road leads to liturgy, the place where the Risen Jesus can be encountered in his eucharistic life. Thus the true encounter of Emmaus is less with the earthly teacher than with the heavenly teacher, although the earthly teacher is a very important part of that encounter. This awareness should help keep teachers' motives pure even if they gain during the process, such as admiration from or lasting friendships with their students.

3. After the students have engaged in both the journey and the eucharistic meeting, they can be expected to turn back toward their point of origin to meet their brothers and sisters on the road to share the Good News. This stage is not something over which the teacher has control. It flows naturally from the journey and meeting.

Mirroring Emmaus, there is less and less of the earthly teacher at each of these stages. In the beginning the traditional instructional role is more critical, though of course it is not an authoritarian one because it begins by a loving discerning of where the students are so as to walk with them. This loving discernment and undertaking of the journey foreshadows the burning hearts that students will eventually experience, when they in turn return to the road to share what they have found.

If the only place where the disciples could recognize Jesus was at the Eucharist, in the quiet place of encounter off the road, away from the bustle of the world, perhaps the liturgy could become the main place where Christian education takes place. The liturgy is, after all, by definition, the point of encounter with Christ, and that encounter is the essence of a sacrament.

Yet Jesus chose that worldly setting in meeting the disciples, and here the Emmaus events may bear much more similarity to the modern world than we might first guess. Although readers of Luke's account may assume that only Jesus and the two disciples were on the road, at that time of year in ancient Israel the journey was most likely far from a quiet one, as Moule explains:

> Probably it was not "rural solitude, charmed into sabbath peace." It was evening, so no longer Sabbath but the beginning of their new week. And it was Passover when vast hosts of pilgrims peopled all the environs of Jerusalem, which were at such seasons busy with an extended range of camps. The road at such a time would be thronged with wayfarers. The two friends would often need to thread their way along, and pick up their talk after a break, amidst the passing and meeting multitudes.[39]

Just like the setting, the disciples, too, were not unlike Christians of today in certain important ways. They had heard the Good News, but they found difficulties, not the least of which was that almost all of them, who had once believed Jesus might be the Messiah, had abandoned him during the last days. The similarity is not complete, of course, because these disciples were living with the founder of Christianity himself—centuries did not distance them from him as they do us. Yet the confusion they suffered when what they thought they understood became problematic was no less difficult than for many today. It is not too much to say that Jesus re-evangelized on the road, and if re-evangelization is

---

[39] Moule, *Emmaus*, 59.

the answer to today's religious instructional problem, what better teacher preparation can we have than to study what happened on those seven miles?

Now the main lines of the Emmaus pedagogy are clarified. But how are we to apply them? A reading of the Emmaus account cannot suffice to put the model into practice. It needs to be reflected on, even lived, in depth, and that is what I hope this inquiry will assist in doing. In Part Two, we will look at each of the ten principles in their scriptural context to extract what Jesus did that is a model of what we in turn could do. In Part Three, we will trace out the specifics even further for liturgically centered catechesis.

Part Two

The Ten Emmaus
Catechetical Principles

The Emmaus Principles

1. Jesus knew who he was.

2. Jesus knew his mission.

3. Jesus approached the disciples in person.

4. Jesus walked along with them.

5. Jesus asked them a question.

6. Jesus said to them, "O foolish [dear witless] ones!"

7. Jesus made as if to go further.

8. Jesus took bread, blessed it, broke it, and distributed it—whereupon their eyes were open.

9. They spoke with each other.

10. They got up immediately and returned to Jerusalem.

1. Jesus Knew Who He Was

We find that, throughout his life on earth, Jesus was in constant touch with his Father, who had sent him. This is why, when he taught, he could do so with authority. A hallmark of his teaching was authority, the force of truth, not learning. He seemed to speak of that which he knew. This was "the irresistible force of a Divine message, delivered under the sense of a Divine mission. Nothing could have been more opposed to the traditionalism of the Scribes...."[1]

There has been debate on how much Jesus knew as a man about his divinity, but it does not really concern us here. What he did know was that he had a divine Father, that he and his Father were one, that he needed time away from worldly affairs in order to be present to the world more fully. Countless publications have been written about Jesus as a teacher—so many that they cannot be summarized here.

---

[1] Swete, *Teaching of Our Lord*, 19.

Each seems to offer yet a new insight into this fascinating topic, one of such value for us who carry on his teaching work.

Unique, unable to be categorized, he was an independent teacher, transcending any particular epoch:

> Great men are, to a considerable degree,
> influenced by the circumstances of their birth,
> land, education, and station; like the planets,
> they pursue a path resulting from the
> centrifugal and centripetal moral forces to
> which they are subjected. Christ pursues one
> which defies all calculation of external
> influences, and of which there is no solution but
> in the throne of God.[2]

His teaching was simple yet far-reaching:

> It is more than primitive innocence and
> goodness. Though visible on earth, its place is
> far in heaven; and to see it, you must look
> through a long colonnade of celestial light. The
> truth he brings is not truth in blossom or in
> fruit, but in seed; not to adorn and wither, but to
> fall into the soul and germinate. Within his
> simplest rule of man's duty are wrapped up the
> grandest principles of God's government; by
> proverbs and examples he sets up guide-boards
> on all the cross-roads in the realm of truth; in
> outline he sketches the map of human
> knowledge, and by hints points us to the details;
> his instructions have been the subject of interest
> for centuries, and they are still of unexhausted
> interest—an unwasting cruse of oil to feed the
> first of mind.[3]

---

[2] Thomson, *Christ as a Teacher*, 14.

[3] Ibid., 8.

Jesus and his teaching were one. For that reason, I find it hard to separate this principle, "Jesus Knew Who He Was," from the next, "Jesus Knew His Mission." His success was due in large part to the fact that he *was* the message, and as Marshall McLuhan said, "The medium is the message." All the more true with Jesus: the more a disciple accepts him and is one with him, the more that person assimilates his message.

In looking at what Jesus was and taught, Genung describes the meaning of living truth as "not the digging-up of some dead and buried fact, but the creation, by means of a vital principle, of a new fact in life."[4] Jesus was in touch with the source of truth.

Breitigam explains this living power of Jesus to draw the attention and will of those who learned from him: "His words were the expression, not only of His own life experience, but of his own character. Not only did he teach the truth, but he was the truth. It was this that gave his teaching, power." [5] Breitigam draws a parallel with the teaching situation today:

> [Students] must not merely see a theory,
> however logical, but the loving character and
> glory of Christ. They must be led to behold the
> riches of the eternal world, until they are
> encouraged, animated, and won. The love of
> Jesus must be the motive of all effort. It impels,
> it constrains, it captivates.[6]

I cannot overestimate the need for every catechist to acknowledge his or her self and to understand it—to know who he or she is. I have occasionally seen an instructor with a weak sense of identity feel threatened by students' ques-

---

4 Genung, *What a Carpenter Did*, 25.

5 Breitigam, *Teacher Sent from God*, 5.

6 Ibid., 50, citing *Counsels on Sabbath School Work*, 52.

tions or stated doubts, or fall apart under the various pressures of life that we all face in our "other" jobs, in our families, in our rectories or other church groups. There is no reason why almost anyone of good will, in the state of grace, and with a little preparation cannot do a fine job as a teacher; but there must be an underlying solid identity. Those in transition, such as recent converts and those from troubled homes, need to "jell" and heal. Let them walk further with Jesus on the Emmaus road first.

2. Jesus Knew His Mission

*A*s mentioned earlier, it is difficult to separate Jesus' knowing who he was from knowing his mission because these are two sides of the same coin. When people know who they are, and when they are unified with their message, they want to share it with others.

Those called to instruction, particularly religious instruction, know they are called by recognizing their love of learning and sharing knowledge. When they study, their inner being resonates. Because of Jesus' constant communication with his Father through prayer, he knew what he had to do. Everything he did attested to that understanding on his part.

Although Jesus had three roles—preacher, healer, and teacher—

> folks did not call him the Preacher...Great
> Healer...but "Good Teacher." The word

> translated "Master" in the Authorized Version
> [of the Bible] means "Teacher."[1]

He was the consummate teacher, a title he easily accepted:

> Jesus was called Teacher more often than any
> other of the many titles by which He was known
> in the days of His earthly ministry. He was called
> Teacher by His disciples, by friends, by strangers,
> by enquirers and even by His enemies.[2]

In the four Gospels, the term *didaskalos* ("teacher") is found to be used over forty times in reference to Jesus; "Rabbi," the standard Jewish title for an eminent scholar, is also found throughout the four Gospels; *epistates* ("schoolmaster" or "superintendent") is used as well, but only by Luke. The verb *didasko* ("teach") is applied in the Gospels forty-five times to events in which Jesus is mentioned.[3]

While he accepted the designation of "Teacher," he forbade his disciples, even those who would teach, to accept it for themselves. He did not create a school of teachers as the Scribes tried to do.[4] What he asked of his disciples was to follow him. He claimed authority to interpret the Law; he claimed respect for his teaching ("whoever is ashamed of me..." [Mt 10, 33]); he claimed the divine origin of his teaching ("the Father Who sent me..." [Jn 14, 24]); he challenged listeners to test the validity of his claim that he spoke not of himself but only what God commanded; he claimed his word was the final authority ("Heaven and earth will pass away..." [Mt 5, 18]); and he claimed to speak words leading to everlasting life.[5]

---

1   Piper, *How Would Jesus Teach?*, 12.

2   Rixon, *How Jesus Taught*, 1.

3   Ibid., 2-3.

4   Swete, *Teaching of Our Lord*, 15.

5   Rixon, *How Jesus Taught*, 3.

With an impassioned need to engage in his mission, he easily attracted the masses:

> Christ was a popular teacher. He attracted the masses....It is only occasionally that any man can get a crowd. No man can hold it long; the multitude, after hearing once or twice, lose their curiosity.[6]

His doctrines were popular—"the words of Christ make light, and make it more and more abound."[7] So too was his style. He spoke as his hearers needed: dialogistically, allegorically, metaphorically. "He so associates truth with the heavens and the earth as to make every thing a memorial of duty, a remembrance of truth, or a reprover of sin."[8]

He was "no respecter of persons," wanting to gather people not because of his partiality but because of their necessities; he was "democratic" in the largest and best sense. He was a human teacher, meek and lowly. When he said he and the Father are one, "it required the greatest humility to make such a pretension."[9]

Although these qualities may seem somewhat passive, they are far from it. When the occasion called for it, Jesus could be strong and commanding, as when he drove out the moneychangers from the Temple (Mk 11, 15-17).

Learning Goals and Objectives

Like any teacher, Jesus used specific learning objectives—immediate and small-scale goals for the student to

---

6 Thomson, *Christ as a Teacher*, 1.

7 Ibid., 2.

8 Ibid., 3.

9 Ibid., 5-7.

attain. These objectives he marshaled into service of larger aims or goals which covered broader concerns. These goals differed earlier and later in his ministry in the same way as the goals of evangelism and catechesis differ. His earlier goals included:

> "To expand and enrich their idea of God, to widen and deepen their sympathies with mankind, to liberate their fears, to remove obsessions, to break down barriers by revealing life in all its fullness, life in the blessed community, life as the Father wills it"; and further, "to kindle a passion for God, to make his righteousness attractive, to enlist in the joyous family of the Kingdom."[10]

Later, his goals changed to help his disciples grasp his true claim in being the suffering savior.

As for Jesus' learning objectives, Piper believes they were basically "to transform the lives of His disciples and through them to transform other lives and regenerate human society," broken up into four smaller ("enabling") objectives:[11]

1. To lead his disciples to trust God completely, and love Him as their Father (Jn 14, 1-2; Mt 6, 25-34; Jn 3, 16)

2. To win them to active faith in himself as the Son of God (Jn 3, 16; Jn 4, 26)

3. To teach the Christian way of life, in contrast to mere formal religion and worldly living (Sermon on the Mount, Beatitudes, Mt 21, 28-30)

---

[10] Canon Charles E. Raven, *Christ and Modern Education*, cited in Piper, *How Would Jesus Teach?*, 30-31.

[11] Piper, *How Would Jesus Teach?*, 32-34.

4. To prepare and train his disciples to be
   active workers, witnesses, and leaders in
   spreading this faith and this way of life
   throughout the world (Mt 4, 19; Mt 28, 19)

Where He Taught

With a universal mission, Jesus taught everywhere:

> A real teacher is a teacher all the time,
> everywhere. The smallest part of our work may
> be done within the walls of a church building,
> even though that is all-important. Jesus
> certainly believed in week-day contacts with his
> pupils! He taught people how to live while they
> were engaged in the normal activities of life. So
> much did he believe in, and engage in, social
> intercourse that when his enemies sought to
> caricature him the worst they could do was to
> call him a glutton and a winebibber. How can
> we teach folks unless we know them, and how
> can we know them unless we share life with
> them?[12]

Long before Emmaus, there was a "journeying" aspect to
the instruction Jesus gave his disciples, as Cary draws out.
As regards his school, it differed from others of his day in
that:

> [P]robably...no others had their classes move
> about so much as did his. Even more than the
> noted school of Aristotle, that of Jesus might
> fittingly have taken the name Peripatetic, and it
> is not without interest to notice that the Greek
> verb from which that name is derived is used
> (John 6:66; 7:1; etc.) to denote the "walking" of
> Jesus and his disciples. They received his

---

[12] Piper, *How Would Jesus Teach?*, 15.

> instructions as they walked with him beside the
> lake, traversed the plains, climbed the
> mountains, or entered the courts of the Temple.
> This going from place to place was partly
> caused by the opposition he met in Capernaum
> and other towns. Another reason for it may
> have been that Jesus, being a prophet as well as
> a teacher, wished to give his message, either
> directly or through his disciples, to people
> throughout the land. Even as a teacher he
> planned for what bore a slight resemblance to
> our systems of university extension.[13]

Jesus thus took his disciples on the prototype of a true educational journey, a living prototype of what some have called the "Christian walk," the coming ever closer to Jesus that is the aim of every catechist to foster in his or her group. That journey is symbolized still more cogently in the Emmaus event and imagery.

Specific Teaching Techniques

Beginning where his audience was, he would attach his teaching to well-known ideas and concepts, using day-to-day opportunities which presented themselves.[14]

He often cited the Hebrew Scriptures, which were also part of his audience's daily life.

His methods were simple but far from simplistic. He used stories, examples, and references to things with which his hearers were familiar. These he couched in simple, concrete words and short, simple sentences, using repetition for greater understanding.[15] He used the question, discussion,

---

[13] Cary, *First Christian School*, 51-52.

[14] Rixon, *How Jesus Taught*, 9.

[15] Schroeder and Slaght, *New Testament Studies*.

and silence method—waiting for a response to an insightful question—or teaching by his own action. He also used object lessons, narratives, and pupil participation,[16] as well as life-related application "projects." He used cases, the developing method, methods geared to gaining attention and appercep-tion, suggestion, analysis and synthesis, induction and deduction.[17]

We also find the use of paradox, epigrams, hyperbole, simile, metaphor, proverbs, methods of argument, even poetry (parallel lines answering each other, contrast, and synthesis).[18] As Piper notes, Jesus was not tied to any one methodology other than that of love, whatever that might entail at the moment. It is easy to see how he changed according to learner needs. With crowds, he condensed lofty truth into parables and stories from everyday experience in simple and symbolic language. How different from dealing with his critics, whom he tried to convince of a truth they opposed or refused to deal with; he often posed questions for which he would then ask for an answer that stymied the audience.[19]

Experiential Learning

One of the best teaching techniques of all is providing the opportunity for experiential learning, and this is a method that Jesus used often:

> Before they [the disciples] could have an
> unshakable faith in him as the Son of God, they

---

[16] Rixon, *How Jesus Taught*, chapters 4 and 5.

[17] Jones, *Teaching Methods of the Master*, in which an entire chapter is devoted to each method.

[18] Rixon, *How Jesus Taught*, chapter 6.

[19] Piper, *How Would Jesus Teach?*, 40.

must have experience with him. There is no
evidence that Jesus pressed the question of their
faith in him until that day at Caesarea Philippi,
when they were discussing the conflicting
current opinions about him. They had then
heard his wonderful teachings, caught his spirit,
been his friends, lived in his presence. They had
discovered him for themselves.[20]

Non-Dogmatization

Jesus did not dogmatize, although few other teachers
have had as good a reason to do so:

> [H]e was not teaching facts; he was teaching
> people to face facts. He was not teaching
> religion; he was teaching people to be religious.
> He was not teaching intellectual assent to
> theological propositions; he was teaching
> people to experience God in their lives. That is
> why he dealt with life situations and constantly
> had in mind the practical needs of his pupils.[21]

While he did teach doctrine, of course, in doing so, he
tried to make the truth experiential. He could abide imperfec-
tion in his learners' attempts:

> Jesus is the perfect teacher because He
> completely understands the value of
> imperfection. He sees and teaches us to see that
> our sense of incompleteness completes us. In
> acknowledging imperfection we are perfected.
> The awareness of absence is presence.
> Repentance is absolution. Forgiving others is to
> be forgiven. Mourning is comforting. Seeking is
> finding. When we completely understand this,

---

20 Piper, *How Would Jesus Teach?*, 25.

21 Ibid., 41-42.

we are full grown. We become the perfected
disciples of the perfect teacher who has
promised to bring us with him into perfect
union with our heavenly Father.[22]

Individualization

Jesus did not treat all his listeners the same:

> As a Teacher Jesus faced teaching situations as
> varied as they were challenging...At times His
> audience was called a multitude; sometimes the
> student group comprising His class were the
> twelve disciples, and on other occasions the
> teaching situation involved one other person in
> addition to Himself, with one or two other
> persons in the background.[23]

Although he delivered his teaching partly in public to the
crowds and partly in private to his disciples, his first and
foremost focus was on the crowd, who always found him a
patient and compassionate teacher. The disciples often
received special instructions after the crowds.[24] As Piper
describes it:

> Jesus had two kinds of students. From a larger
> group of disciples, He chose a smaller group of
> 70 disciples as well as the Twelve to be set apart
> for special training (Mk 3,13). But this larger
> group still followed Him even after the Twelve
> were chosen, and were with him during most of
> His ministry.[25]

---

[22] Lever, *Perfect Teacher*, 123-124.

[23] Rixon, *How Jesus Taught*, 5.

[24] Swete, *Teaching of Our Lord*, 19.

[25] Piper, *How Would Jesus Teach?*, 21-22.

Thus we see that while Jesus had a small special training class of twelve members, there was a larger group of pupils numbering more than seventy; and there was a still larger group who might be said to be on the outer fringe of discipleship, a sort of extension class, less regular, less active, some of whom no doubt were Jesus' sincere pupils while he was in their home village, but who did not or could not follow him about. The Twelve were a class within a class, a smaller circle within two larger ones.

Affectivity

The disciples were different from each other but shared the same geographical origins in Galilee and thus similar understanding and camaraderie. Jesus' group of students was blessed by high morale; good teacher that he was, he had arranged for this. Such camaraderie would allow creation of the family of faith more easily. Similarly, he had a personal love for each student:

> Jesus did not simply teach a class, he taught
> Peter, and Andrew, and James, and John. They
> had his individual attention. Without this deep
> understanding of each of them personally Peter
> would never have been restored after his denial,
> Thomas might have died a doubter, Philip
> would never have grasped the truth that to
> know Jesus was to know the Father.[26]

There is a vast affective difference between preparing a lesson to teach to a class and preparing to teach individuals. The latter requires insight into the special needs, weaknesses, aptitudes of each member; it also requires special preparation of the lesson so as to apply it to each member, awakening

---

[26] Piper, *How Would Jesus Teach?*, 26.

each one's aptitude, overcoming each weakness, meeting each need.

"Teachers who carry their pupils upon their hearts and pray without ceasing for their salvation will be soul-winning teachers," Breitigam remarks, noting that:

> Christ, the peerless Teacher, set us an example of how to pray, how to live the prayer life, and how a teacher sent from God will have a real burden for souls. Because His life was one of constant communion with God, He was endued with power from on high, and His teaching ministry was ever filled with power.[27]

How could such love on the part of the teacher be fostered? Cary notes that one striking feature of Jesus' teaching was the close companionship of teacher and pupils, developing the affective dimension. Under such conditions the relationship was more like a family than a formal classroom, a situation which broke a Jewish tradition about how a teacher should relate to the students:

> When the right men were associated in this way, their hearts became so closely knit together that the relation between them was more like that of a parent to his children than like that which exists at the present day between a professor and his students. It was like that of Paul and Timothy: the teacher regarding the young man as a well-beloved son, and the student reverencing his teacher as one whose "teaching, conduct, purpose, faith, longsuffering, love, patience" (Timothy 3:10) he ought to imitate.
> ...They were like a family, sharing their purse, their food, their joys, their sorrows. His conduct was not in full accord with the precepts of one

---

27 Breitigam, *Teacher Sent from God*, 95.

of the Talmudists who said that a teacher
"should beware of compromising his dignity
before his pupils; he should not jest, nor should
he eat or drink in their presence."[28]

In developing the affective dimension of his learners to
weather the storms of adversity:

Our Lord was an educator as well as an
instructor. He wished men to embrace His
teaching not merely intellectually but also—and
especially—affectively. He knew that the will is
the driving power of the soul and that an
undisciplined will often misguides an
enlightened mind.[29]

It was in his teaching about the Eucharist that Jesus'
special gift as a teacher was clear:

[N]owhere does the pedagogy of this Teacher
shine more brilliantly than in His efforts to
show us the importance of the Eucharist as
food. The foundation was laid by miraculously
supplying the loaves and fishes to feed the
hungry thousands. They were thrilled and
imagined that again material abundance was in
sight for the Jews. But Jesus had something else
in view.[30]

The crowd found it hard to accept when he said that the
bread he would give would be his flesh. But because they had
seen that he could provide materially, they chose to listen
further. At the Last Supper, after he taught about the Eucharist,
the apostles no longer found it a hard saying to accept.[31]

---

[28] Cary, *First Christian School*, 53.

[29] Bandas, *Catechetics in the New Testament*, 17.

[30] Russell, *Jesus the Divine Teacher*, 238.

[31] Ibid.

Reliance on Others to
Spread His Message

Jesus left much of the teaching methodology of the Good News up to his chosen ones, commissioning them simply to go and teach in his name. We don't know if he gave any specific directions for exactly how to do this. Ellis considers it another proof of the greatness of Jesus as a teacher that he taught in oral words and thus depended on others and their personal influence to spread his message:

> No greater words were ever spoken by any teacher than the following request of Jesus given to his twelve chosen students: "Go ye therefore and teach all nations...teaching them to observe all things whatsoever I have commanded you."[32]

"The Teacher's Last Lesson," to use Jones' term, was liturgical in nature, a totally integrated lesson indeed. It was with his twelve best friends, those he planned to send forward with his message after his death and resurrection. The teacher thus taught the lesson as a friend rather than a formal teacher, yet that did not take away from the lesson's power.

With this background of Jesus as one who knew his mission and who was well prepared as a teacher, we can understand him in that capacity on the Emmaus road.

---

[32] Ellis, *Jesus, the Great Teacher*, 14.

3. Jesus Approached the Disciples in Person

*A*s Buisson explains in starting off his inquiry, Jesus does not wait for the disciples at the end of the Emmaus road. Instead, he comes searching for them near the start of their journey. Seeing the sad, discouraged disciples returning home with dashed hope, he approaches them. He takes the loving initiative. The approach of Jesus was indeed, as Gillièron puts it:

> [A]n unusual initiative. Luke focuses his reader at the outset on the identity of the Stranger. He could have treated it later or postponed it till the end of the narrative, as in a good novel, the discovery of the mystery. But Jesus—for it is He—is not a fictional person. He approaches. This sums up everything.
>
> ...Luke means by the formula, which he uses elsewhere in a similar circumstance, that he arrives when...The moment is important. The

> disciples were alone and yet not alone. Jesus approached. He had not been there, now He is. It is a surprising event, which swerves the course of history....
>
> It is precisely at this moment when the conversation seemed to be sinking that Jesus rejoined them. His coming is delayed, always to the despair of His own. It is not that He likes to see us at an impasse in order to come to us. We say that...when He comes to us, He comes to our aid, spontaneously, without our needing to call on Him.[1]

Buisson notes that the first step of education in developing faith is a step of authentic love. It is love that gives us the desire to search. This is normal, for love is the sign *par excellence* of Christ. It is love that starts off the search.[2]

So we conclude that those to be helped on their journey of search must be certain that there is love in their instructor's heart. Those to be helped must feel this love through a uniquely personal experience, not through words alone. It is not enough that the teacher is capable of loving. Students must see it through concrete gestures, and they must be in touch with their teacher.[3]

Certainly the disciples of Emmaus were in touch with Christ. He drew close to them. His love was manifested by gesture: his approach and his continuing along the road with them. What an unobtrusive approach it was! He could have overwhelmed them with retinues of angels, a theological discourse, or even reproach for not having stood by Him during the events of Good Friday. From this simple, personal approach, he set the stage for a whole catechesis. It is an

---

[1] Gillièron, *Le Repas d'Emmaüs, 16-18.*

[2] Buisson, "Le Christ," 67.

[3] Ibid., 68.

example for us, as we are always tempted to think of religion as doctrine or morality, whereas Christianity is *someone*. To make this presence visible, we must follow his example and make our approach through love. Our approach must be authentic, or else others will sense it is not, back off, and set up new boundaries.[4]

When a teacher approaches in the name of religion, students are all the quicker to sense how authentic is the love that motivates the approach. Most of us can recall encounters, informal or formal, when we were on the receiving end of a faith-sharing mission that somehow made us feel threatened because the approach did not seem genuine and coming from *agape* love.

The disciples on the road to Emmaus apparently felt open when the stranger approached them, just as they had when he first came into their lives long before. There was something about this man's approach that touched the heart inexplicably and drew others onward.

The disciples were not only in need of catechesis but also re-evangelization, and that is what Jesus came to provide them. They had heard the original message that Jesus would die and rise again. This was not the first time they had to deal with the doctrine of the resurrection, but their faith had been challenged between the first time they had heard it and now. They could not walk around the difficulties on their own, so they walked back instead. In this they are something of a prototype of many of today's faithful.

Thus Jesus is a model for us not only as catechists but as re-evangelizers, showing the close link between catechesis and evangelization in an ever-deepening faith process.

---

4 Buisson, "Le Christ," 68.

4. Jesus Walked Along with Them

*J*esus did not just meet the two disciples, stay awhile, then go his way. The disciples were putting more and more distance—in every sense of the word—between themselves and Jerusalem. They had turned their back on their home, returning to the life they had left, and Jesus now walked with them, as Buisson explains.

This step toward Emmaus represents the core mystery of faith: the Incarnation, God-become-man. Jesus journeyed with his people. He was the carpenter of Nazareth, a man with a particular profession who lived in a particular land. He shared his life with people to the extent of their miseries and struggles against mediocrity.

Although there was a law in ancient Israel that said pupils must put their teachers above their parents in providing for their needs, Jesus—the teacher of teachers—had no place to call his permanent home, and apparently wished none. Even though he was the Son of God, he divested himself of his glory to pitch his tent among his people. He truly walked with them.

For each person, Christ took on an aspect which could make a relationship possible. He became all to all, as St. Paul would say later. This is quite different from a desire to please or an attempt to fit in because Jesus' concern was for the welfare of the other person, not for his own personal gain. He had to spend time with his students so that he and they would become comfortable together.

I have certainly found this Emmaus principle true in my own life. To educate people in faith—and I find this true whether they are old or young—does not mean to merely give them a course or a lesson. It means to experience and share interest in their lives, including their leisure activities. It means to participate in their efforts and their inquiries; it means, above all, to understand who they are.

To use the imagery of the road, engaging in catechesis means becoming a fellow traveler. The basic identity of Christians is that we are brothers and sisters; even if we religious instructors are older or wiser or more mature in faith than our students, we are still on the road ourselves. Our own search can serve as a good role model for our students.

We need not always have the answers. In fact, we cannot expect to, not even in matters of religion, not even in a Church promised divine guidance by its founder. We must remember, for starters, that there are some mysteries God has not revealed (Jn 16, 12). There are also some which require a great deal of wrestling-with from us, like Jacob and the angel did in the Hebrew Scriptures.

I think it is very helpful for our students to grasp this fact—that we, their teachers, are also fellow travelers. Although we may be handing on a religious tradition, we are, like them, simply members of the faithful. A Roman collar, a

Sister's crucifix, or a lay catechist's certificate are merely signs of deep commitment to living life on the road as followers of the Master Teacher and to sharing the Good News with our brothers and sisters.

But catechists may often have good intentions and yet seem to have little success, as they see it. Why don't students always recognize good will on the part of the teacher? Perhaps for the same reason the disciples could not recognize Jesus on the road to Emmaus. Gillièron explains:

> It was not He who had changed, but they. They saw Him, but still overcome by the impact of events which had occurred at Jerusalem, they could not make out His true identity. For them, Jesus is He who had just been crucified. He is thus the Disappeared, not the Living. How could He then be there now, walking with them?[1]

From this aspect of Emmaus, we who catechize can see that we shouldn't necessarily count our efforts in vain if success is not forthcoming. Success will probably come down the road if we follow through on our mutual journey with our students—not just by identifying where they are but also by finding out exactly where *they* think they are.

---

[1]   Gillièron, *Le Repas d'Emmaus*, 20.

5. Jesus Asked the Disciples a Question

What a beautiful example we teachers have here! Once again, Christ did not put himself in the center. He—though the Son of God, though the Master Teacher—did not say, for instance, "Here I am to bring you the light." He didn't even ask, "Don't you recognize me?" After all, they had traveled together before. Perhaps he was more amused than displeased at their blindness anyway. Instead, he posed a question: "What are you discussing on your way?" Imagine! As if he didn't know!

His question came only after walking with them for a while, yet they took him for a traveler—as Buisson notes in delineating this stage—and his question responded to the disciples' need, as they were still reeling under the shock of the recent events. They needed to talk it out. One commented, perhaps with a tinge of sarcasm, "Are you the only resident of Jerusalem who does not know the things that went on there the last few days?"

This answer did not throw Jesus. He continued his line of inquiry, echoing the disciple's own words when he answered the question with a question, "What things?" In this way he became a listener. He did not present himself as a teacher with superior knowledge. He listened to the story of his own Passion as lived by the disciples. He let the disciples express their feelings, their lost hope, their confusion at the cognitive dissonance caused by reports from the women about the empty tomb confusing their own observations at Calvary. This stage of the journey was not the right point at which to ask them to accept the truth of what had really happened. Only later would he invite them to make a decision about that.

What impresses Gillièron in the way Jesus handles the situation is his excellent teaching approach:

> [He] invites the disciples to explain themselves, to unveil their real situation gradually and to the measure that they would expose it. Jesus certainly did not need to hear them to know where they were. But they did. For it is in speaking that we come to understand what we wish to say, to discover where we are.[1]

Luke provides a clue, as Gillièron notes:

> The word used by Luke, *to explain*, shows rather that Jesus chose the pages which, up to now, had scarcely been read in relationship to the Messiah. But these are the pages which permit discovery of the fine points of God's plan. It is an exemplary method, which aims to restore a holistic rather than a partial reading and thus a biased view of the Scriptures. On allowing

---

[1] Gillièron, *Le Repas d'Emmaüs*, 21.

ourselves to be led, we discover who is the
Messiah, and we see that Jesus was truly He.[2]

Soeur Jeanne d'Arc also highlights the catechetical
uniqueness of the way Jesus acted here toward his disciples:

> It is really amazing that He does not give them
> at this moment any other content, anything that
> resembles catechesis, on the way, nor an
> explanation of all that concerns the prophecies;
> He says nothing else than reference to His own
> words and the sacred texts.
>
> Here, He opens their understanding to
> penetrate the Scriptures, He opens their
> understanding of the Scriptures, He gives this
> intimate penetration, this light which allows the
> grasping of the sense, entry into the depth and
> at the same time savoring the taste.
>
> To open Scripture is already to make the
> heart burn; the two had experienced this. Here,
> the complementary action, a divine gift of grace;
> in place of explaining Himself, as He had done
> on the way, He opens the spirit of the apostles
> to the understanding of the Scriptures. From
> now on it is up to them and those who would
> come after the task of deciphering and
> interpreting, not just those called the Twelve
> Apostles by title (now temporarily the
> Eleven)....It is to the entire Church that this
> work of penetrating and elucidating would
> continue throughout the centuries till the end of
> time, each generation utilizing the best
> instruments of their epoch to make it better
> resound and assimilate the inexhaustible Word.[3]

Throughout the Christian Scriptures, Jesus was always
the one who took the initiative with many others in need.

---

2 Gillièron, *Le Repas d'Emmaüs*, 30-31.

3 Jeanne d'Arc, *Les Pélerins d'Emmaüs*, 118-119.

Thus, as Buisson notes, the disciples were truly the point of the Teacher's departure, not himself:

> He restrained Himself from acting as a teacher might be expected to, and in this way showed Himself the teacher of highest caliber. This is true because it is a student's role as well: a loving learning from others what they need, then meeting that need. The teacher thus becomes a student in the process in order to teach well.[4]

By contrast, how often we catechists sally forth to make our points, irrespective of our students' needs! We cannot hold ourselves back. Is it that we value our students so much less than our message? Perhaps we fail to realize how much *we* are the message, rather than our words, to our students.

When I stop to find out where my students are coming from, when I take my direction from there, I see and feel the difference palpably. Sometimes the students tell me they do, too. But I have to be honest and admit that making the students my point of departure slows me down. Perhaps I could achieve more by forging ahead full speed to cover my course syllabus, my lesson plan, my words of wisdom, without my "wasting time" to find out where my students are. With time constraints, this is all the more a temptation. Yet if I don't make the students my departure point, I risk that, at the end, my students would merely be regurgitating my words. I don't want parrots. I want songbirds, and songs come as a loving response to a loving initiative. My restraint is a small sacrifice, perhaps like a tithe or a seed. My investment of time up front in the learning process actually accomplishes more in the long run.

When teachers realize that their students' most important need is to be understood rather than given information,

---

4   Buisson, "Le Christ," 69.

they can appreciate the overarching need to listen to them attentively rather than breaking in without being invited. Here again, this is as important with older and even adult students as it is with younger ones. It was through Jesus' understanding of that need that the consciousness of the disciples was opened.

A receptive, listening attitude can perceive what is going on behind that door and act accordingly. So it was with Christ. His question and patient listening discovered the way to reach the hearts of the disciples. If teachers are really receptive, says Buisson, they would be surprised to discover that the Lord is already at work in the consciousness of their students.[5] He, after all, has been traveling with the students from their birth. The teacher has only recently come into their lives. The Lord is present even when the teacher learns something difficult to accept about students. For instance, as Buisson points out, if young people mention the unfortunate news of having a live-in lover, this sharing means that they are searching, perhaps unconsciously, for the Absolute and the Limitless, as was the Samaritan woman in her successive experiences. Yet despite her misguided behavior, Jesus picked her out as one of his few students to raise to understanding his messiahship.

In this need for teachers to recognize the Lord's work in the students, I wholeheartedly agree with Buisson. When my own students share, even flaunt, some morally questionable aspect of their lives, my casual comment, "Oh?" rather than a horrified gasp or hasty quotation from the Magisterium often disarms them and they begin to open up. Thus we can continue the journey.

We teachers really must be careful about judging. Like Jesus, we will be walking with others who have their particular mix of joys, sufferings, hopes, and sins. But we come

---

5   Buisson, "Le Christ," 69.

with our own, and so we must never forget we are exactly like our students. With this realization, the distances between teacher and students melt. Still, the road to Emmaus leads on.

6. Jesus Said to Them, "O Foolish Ones!"

*T*he time had come when Jesus could explain what the disciples needed to know, but he had to help them realize how far off the mark they had been. "How slow you are to believe all that the prophets have announced!" Although this line has often been translated as "O fools!" or "O foolish ones" (King James Version) or as "What little sense you have" (New American Bible), a softer wording perhaps more closely approaches what Jesus was trying to convey, as Moule believes:

> Is it presumptuous to think that when, to His
> now eager listeners, He proceeded to unfold the
> prophecies, His friendly license was
> accompanied by a smile of joy? In our noble
> Authorized Version, we can only regret the blot
> made by the rendering, "O fools!" Rather, "Dear
> witless ones!" I seem to hear anything but a

> critic's censure. It is rather the accent of a friend,
> delighted to take their part against themselves,
> to hold up their mistake to them as a matter for
> the happy laughter of those who see a dour
> delusion vanish into joy. I picture to myself a
> radiant smile upon the face of the Lord as He
> begins the long monologue which is to kindle
> their hearts into such a fire.[1]

Having discovered the disciples' need, only then would Jesus move into a teaching mode, as Buisson comments about this stage. These disciples had failed to fathom any better than most of his other followers that the Messiah would be sacrificed, not honored on a golden throne. They just "didn't get it," as we say today.

But now the time had come for the proclamation of the Word of God. Jesus helped the disciples to see the light of the paschal mystery in this journey. "Did not the Messiah have to undergo all this so as to enter into his glory?" He began with Moses, then all the prophets, and as they walked on he interpreted for them every passage of Scripture which referred to him.

With a touch of humor, Gillièron asks about the disciples' reactions to this Scripture lesson from their unknown traveling companion:

> Can we imagine what effect that must have
> produced? Perhaps through discretion, perhaps
> through respect for the disciples of Emmaus,
> Luke abstains from commenting that this
> scarcely convinced them. When men are at that
> point, overcome by Jesus' death, Biblical study
> is not enough. Even the clearest reading of the
> Bible will never raise to his feet someone lying
> prone on the ground.

---

[1] Moule, *Emmaus*, 43-44.

> Meanwhile, the disciples...were not totally
> insensible to that exceptional Scripture study.
> They soon would declare..."Were not our hearts
> burning within us when He spoke to us along
> the way and opened the Scriptures for us?"[2]

As Buisson points out, the Word of God is not a pure and simple teaching given from the outside. It is revelation, and that comes from within, shedding light and moving our intuition. What the Word revealed to the two disciples was the reality of the experience they had undergone. It gave them a positive view of the experience through which they had passed, leading them from confusion to peace.

The light which the two disciples of Emmaus received was thus not something outside and foreign to themselves. It was their own life, their own experience, that Christ enlightened and clarified. There is a line in the popular hymn "Amazing Grace" that sums it up well: "I once was lost, but now am found, was blind, but now I see." This kind of light brings not only understanding but gratitude.

A look back along the Emmaus road helps us see how well Jesus prepared his disciples for this moment of insight. If we—or Luke—left out the earlier stages of the Emmaus journey, it would seem that Jesus was simply engaging in religious teaching and perhaps reproaching his students for their lack of understanding. Surely the Holy Spirit was guiding Luke to include the earlier stages of the journey so that we could appreciate the preparation for the teachable moment. It doesn't work merely to throw the Word of God like seeds on just any kind of ground, because the soil has to accept it. Gardeners know this. Poorly prepared soil produces a poor harvest. But the disciples were well prepared. The Word had been carefully planted.

---

2 Gillièron, *Le Repas de Emmaüs*, 33.

What must have been the thoughts coursing through the disciples as the Master Teacher taught! Even on ordinary occasions, the road was probably rather boring, but *this* journey had commenced in overwhelming discouragement. It was certainly not one the disciples wished to make. Yet they were becoming absolutely fascinated and, as the day and the miles went on, walking in brighter inner light than even the hot Israeli sun bearing down on them. Did the paradox occur to them that the stranger, far from being one in the dark, as he had first seemed, had brought that light?

Sometimes, if we are lucky, our students may have the same experience as the disciples on the road. We teachers, particularly of religion, may seem old-fashioned and thus terribly unenlightened. But if we pass through all the earlier stages, eventually the students' inner light will shine. Perhaps then they may recognize us for our role—if not, however, no matter, because they recognize the truth. Perhaps, too, they may thank us for our part; but if not, again, it does not matter. At this stage, we teachers have done all our work, and the next step is up to them.

7. Jesus Made as if to Go Further

*H*ere, notes Buisson about this stage, is the decisive moment in the disciples' journey toward faith. They had received light from above. Having taught them what he had to say, he waited for their response. It was up to them to decide what they were going to do about what they had heard.

Jesus did not impose himself, so he continued his journey with them but also began a process of leave-taking. Perhaps he simply moved a few steps ahead. Perhaps he said "good-bye." The decision was all up to them now. Would they keep him or let him go? As Guitton describes the incident:

> But Christ, now glorious and seated near the
> Father, does not leave His land, His friends, or
> His work. He takes His place among His group.
> He does not want faith in the resurrection to be
> imposed. He respects the meanderings of the

> souls on the road leading toward Emmaus for
> the entire two hours. He provides the two
> disciples with an explanation of Biblical history,
> for which He gives the meaning, going from one
> exalted level to another as a true teacher. En
> route, He reveals the secret of existence to them,
> the meaning of evil and darkness. And while
> the Spirit radiates, He "burns" their hearts.[1]

His humanity, at this point outside the material world, is nonetheless fully present at this place in space and time. Yet it possesses time and space; it is not possessed by them. But it is so familiar; it seems to have increased in proximity. This companion of the road has no hurried air; he has plenty of time. He wishes faith to be strengthened by a prolonged experience:

> And thus He waited to see what the disciples
> would do. They could have remained where
> they were and let Jesus continue His journey as
> they came near Emmaus. He would have gone,
> and they would have been alone as evening
> approached. The disciples did not let Jesus go,
> but pressed Him, noting the time it was getting
> to be: "Stay with us. It is nearly evening. The
> day is practically over."[2]

They made the final decision that no one else could make for them. "Stay with us, Lord." Their response was spontaneous. It was also a prayer. They still did not know that it was Jesus, but they already had a presentiment of him. Their hearts' intuition preceded explicit consciousness, which was not far away.

Moule paints a charming picture of this scene:

---

[1] Guitton, "Les Disciples d'Emmaüs," 159.

[2] Buisson, "Le Christ," 70.

And when this scene shuts, it shuts upon "this
same Jesus" true to His undying friendship still.
The sun is setting, and here is the village. Will
He not stay with them and share their simple
supper? Yes, the disguised King of Immortality
consents at once, and proves delightfully
companionable. He is quite ready to take His
couch beside them, to break the broad thin cake
and bless it as He had done so often in His
mortal days.[3]

What a compelling model for catechists! Like Jesus, we
teachers also address not just a category of people called
"students" but free persons with their own destiny, their own
home in heaven. We cannot make decisions for them once
we have given them the basic information and explanation
to meet their needs. We cannot choose for them, even if their
choices may turn out to be unfortunate ones. To create pres-
sure or take advantage of our authority would be to go
against the whole purpose of education, which is to lead, not
force, out of the darkness of ignorance, frailty, and fear. To
restrain ourselves can sometimes be very difficult for us. Out
of concern, we want to ensure the better choice. But he who
called himself the Way does not. He invites and waits for a
response.

I think many catechists these days are more aware than
ever that they need to invite their students, but what they do
not always understand is that very often the students' decisions will be delayed—and that those decisions may be
perfectly all right. I believe that if we take Jesus on the road
to Emmaus as a model, we can in turn take heart in our
attempts to respect the freedom he created, knowing that the
turning point may come further down the road for the students, even if we are not there to see it.

---

[3] Moule, *Emmaus*, 44.

Here is where an understanding of human development is so important: our student's readiness to respond may not be at the point where we teachers meet them. Here is where our own faith is challenged. We must trust the divine teacher. After all, we who are active in catechesis are really only aides to the Master Teacher. It is his classroom, after all.

8. He Took Bread, Blessed, Broke and Distributed It

With the breaking of the bread, their eyes were opened and they recognized him. For Buisson, this is the sublime moment when the students at last realized what the lesson was all about. Gillièron describes this scene:

> They were thus seated at table, and He with them. All is ready. We might say that the meal had been prepared for a long time, since eternity. Besides, if we are at Emmaus, in Cleophas' house, everything must have seemed that indeed they were around the table of the Lord (1 Cor 10,21) to celebrate the Lord's meal (1 Cor 11,20). These expressions which served the primitive communities well show that it is a communitarian meal when the Resurrected calls His disciples together.[1]

---

[1] Gillièron, *Le Repas d'Emmaüs*, 37-38.

In the Eucharist at Emmaus with his friends, Jesus could draw on the celebration of the liturgy that, since his death and resurrection, would now be celebrated in heaven for all time as well. Gillièron continues, explaining the significance of this Eucharist:

> Here in pronouncing the prayer of blessing at Emmaus, at the very moment when He takes the bread, Jesus places the meal under the sign of what God just accomplished by His ministry, death, and resurrection. The whole meal becomes the place where all God's work in Jesus is represented; that is to say, made present, actualized. The prayer of blessing transfigures the meal. It makes of the simple nourishing meal the Lord's meal, where He takes the food we eat to lead us to the salvation He brought us.[2]

The Eucharist is the place Jesus established for encounter between us and him. He asked us to "do this in remembrance" (Lk 22, 19) of him, but he did not mean it to be done as a mere formality. He meant it to be the place where he could show himself to us and carry out his work in our midst. The Passover celebration, at which the Eucharist was born, is similarly a model of the past made alive in the present. To this day, Jews believe that not just their ancestors but they themselves were personally delivered at the Passover. The feast is the meeting place of all Jews, past, present, and future. So too is the eucharistic feast for all Christians.

Jesus did more than merely take and bless the bread; he broke it to distribute it. The eucharistic meal symbolizes eating as well as feeling totally satisfied, as did the Jewish exiles crossing the desert to the Promised Land centuries earlier, when every morning they received manna "endowed with all delights and conforming to every taste" (Wis 16, 20).

---

2 Gillièron, *Le Repas d'Emmaüs*, 39-40.

But at the Eucharist, it is not just bread that is broken. Gillièron continues with his analysis of the Emmaus Eucharist:

> In distributing the pieces of bread, Jesus breaks
> Himself among His disciples. The hand He
> extends to them is inseparable from the bread it
> distributes...the two disciples around the table
> find themselves engaged in communion with
> Him Who surpasses everything for which they
> had ever hoped when they invited, even
> pressed, Him to come under their roof.[3]

In Israel, meals had always been an act of communion linking the participants in a common destiny. But here, because Jesus' action is mixed with the breaking of the bread, it is not the meal alone that unites them. Jesus creates between himself and them more than a table community: it is a personal community. The disciples participate in himself. In receiving the bread, it is he whom they receive.

We might wonder, as no doubt did the disciples, why Jesus disappeared after the eucharistic meal. Here he had just shared himself most intimately, here the mystery of the stranger on the road was unveiled, and now he was gone. But this disappearance was part of his ongoing catechetical approach at Emmaus. Moule explains:

> He vanishes...leaving them, as to their senses,
> for a little while alone. But this was only that He
> might begin to train them to faith without sight,
> while He went away to reappear in another
> scene. Evidently they were not in the least
> "terrified and affrighted," only delightfully
> awakened to the fulness of their bliss and
> consciousness of what He was who had made it
> for them, then to the compelling need to share it
> with their companions.[4]

---

3 Gillièron, *Le Repas d'Emmaüs*, 42.

4 Moule, *Emmaus*, 45.

Although the students were united with their teacher at the end of the journey, He left because it was time for him to go. He would meet them again in the kingdom, in the unending eternal celebration where all would be revealed and there would be no more journeys of faith. Good teachers always know when to leave. The moment comes when it is time for their students to practice what they have learned.

Secular teachers, especially those trained to foster "learner control," would point out that as the learning process goes on, the teacher's role should change to become less of a traditional instructor and more of a mentor or coach, someone who advises and roots on the sidelines. The students can then take on more responsibility for their own learning.

I think we catechists can find in the Emmaus Eucharist a particularly relevant model for our work. If we have led our students well through the earlier stages, they will be prepared to meet the eucharistic Jesus who communes with his followers at the depths of the heart and soul but is rarely seen directly this side of paradise—and if he is, he usually disappears shortly after giving a foretaste of what awaits at the end of the life journey.

In one sense, the Emmaus journey ends here at the liturgy, yet it does not; once again the students make a move. They need to discuss among themselves what has gone on, to express, to sort out, to decide where to go from here.

Why was it only at the eucharistic meal that the disciples recognized Jesus, since they had not recognized him on the road? It had something to do with the very nature of the Eucharist, as Gillièron understands it:

> The disciples wanted to make the account of it.
> But they did not say how they recognized the
> risen Christ. They say how He made Himself
> known to them. The inversion is full of their
> entire experience. The account goes beyond
> facts. They re-read the events with totally new

> eyes able to discern the Lord's intervention.
> Now they know what they did not know: that
> God, through Christ, had come to them, and that
> He would come again and everywhere to them.
> But what had this meal really been? The
> historians have wondered if it could have been
> the supper. This question is not at all out of the
> question if we consider that Luke did not
> consider it necessary to discuss the meal in the
> terms which he had used to present the Last
> Supper in Jerusalem on the eve of the
> crucifixion (Lk 22, 14ff). Nonetheless,
> throughout his account, beginning with the
> expression the breaking of the bread, which he
> uses regularly to refer to the supper...he shows
> that it was not a matter of the occurrence at
> Emmaus of some meal but the meal of the Lord.
> Could it have been otherwise? For it is there,
> and nowhere else, that the Lord made Himself
> known. For it is there that our closed eyes are
> opened, and that we always recognize Him.[5]

The real reason the disciples recognized Jesus only at the eucharistic meal, however, is that their recognition came in the very act of the breaking of the bread. Nothing else is reported as having taken place there that would explain it. Luke often points out that events in Jesus' ministry took place at sacred meals, which were so much a part of the Jewish tradition. Luke foreshadows the great meal in the kingdom at the end of time; he means to show how, with each meal, the kingdom of the Lord breaks into human history, gathering his community. But Jesus here is a host, and as such he invites and waits for response.

In his analysis of the eucharistic event at Emmaus, Gillièron gives several warnings. First, because the Word of God and the meal of the Lord call for each other, if the one

---

5   Gillièron, *Le Repas d'Emmaüs*, 58-59.

occurs in the absence of the other, the balance, the harmony, is lost. If the Word is preached without the meal, there is only a beautiful commentary or sermon. If the meal is held without the Word, there is only a beautiful feast or celebration. In either case, the faithful would leave as they came, unfulfilled. There are two further risks:

> [It is] a risk of faith, where doubt always seems to come from outside, but where we must accept that it is part of faith, and following Christ. It is for this reason that the believers, in imitation of their brothers below, will always be en route.
>
> But [it is] a risk of faith—if this can be said—in yet another sense: the believer who is sent, one day, on the road with Christ must wait to see Christ coming to him, meeting him where he is. There, more a means of fleeing than evading. More a means of extricating oneself with alibis. When the Risen Lord approaches, He wants us to go with Him all the way to the end, whatever the price, whatever the consequences.[6]

Gillièron concludes:

> Those who do not recognize Christ do not recognize the possibilities given to them; they doubt themselves as much as they doubt Him; they resist His appeal, Give them to eat yourselves.
>
> But let them finish by giving Him the little they have; may they entreat Him to enter, Stay with us. Let the Lord take the bread and break it; then their eyes open even though at the same time their legs droop, their hands are limp, and their lips are dry.[7]

---

[6] Gillièron, *Le Repas d'Emmaüs*, 57.

[7] Ibid., 69.

In retrospect, the Emmaus events gave us a model for eucharistic liturgy. First come the scriptural readings and commentary to prepare the worshipers by bringing the Word. This preparation enkindles the worshipers' hearts for the Lord's eucharistic presence, at which point their eyes are open to see and welcome him. Our worship recalls not only the historical events but also the most sublime knowledge that occurs through the living stream of faith across the centuries, linking worshipers at both the earthly and the heavenly liturgy. How much do we catechists help our students to understand this linking through liturgy, to appreciate our double citizenship in the world and in heaven? Or rather, how much do we understand it ourselves and how do we desire it?

9. They Spoke with Each Other

"Were not our hearts burning inside us as he talked to us on the road and explained the scripture to us?" the disciples asked each other rhetorically.

Of course they were! Buisson finds burning hearts to be the natural consequence of having experienced the risen Jesus. It was in this light that the learners of Emmaus engaged in discussion.

Now the disciples understood what they had gone through, the meaning of their groping, their searching. The Lord was there all along, but they had not known it. Their faith became solid because of the friendly exchange between themselves and Jesus at each stage of the journey.

Their faith was tested once more by his second leave-taking from their midst. In this regard, Gillièron's thoughts are instructive, as he draws out the implications of the paradox that the disciples were once again alone but that he was still with them. Despite the distance that separated them and him, despite the distance that would separate all his disciples and himself throughout the centuries—this includes us!— there would always be the Eucharist. It is indeed a paradox, as Gillièron notes:

> Jesus went off to Heaven...yet He untiringly approaches those who are on the way, His disciples. It is a paradox in tension: awaiting for His triumphal coming on the last day, awaiting for the day when He will visibly show Himself for all time...we must accept that He will be invisible, that our eyes await the hour when they are unobstructed from seeing Him....We are already saved, but saved in hope. But to see what we hope for is to hope no longer... Meanwhile, to hope for what we do not see is to wait in perseverance....[1]

Precisely because the risen one is invisible, the celebration of his meal each Sunday is all the more indispensable. If we never take part in the Eucharist, we will not recognize him, and we will be reduced to being mere being guests or attendees. Nothing would link us to him and to each other except our being in the same place at the same time. Faith made Jesus' invisibility no insurmountable barrier to the disciples. Gillièron continues:

> [T]hey were not without faith, our brothers at Emmaus....They now rejoice. Their eyes do not see? What does that matter! They do better than see; they recognized Him. In the wink of an eye, with the speed of lightning. It was enough for them. It will be enough for us always.[2]

Thus they relived all that happened to them on the road and re-read that page of their life. They reinterpreted, from

---

[1] Gillièron, *Le Repas d'Emmaüs*, 47-48.

[2] Ibid., 48-49.

the point of departure to the striking event of the meal, that which they had not understood. Thus the biblical study to which the stranger had invited them was now "set off in relief," as the metalworking technique that portrays a scene dramatically by elevating it from its background is called. They declared in retrospect their unspeakable suffering of not being able to understand what he had been saying to them: "Were not our hearts burning within us while he spoke to us on the road and opened the scriptures?"

Students of all ages need to reflect on their lives together with others who share the same vantage point, the same challenges, and certainly those who have shared the same meal.[3] To do this is natural; it often occurs even if we teachers do not build in an opportunity for it. But surely Jesus had planned for it at this point at Emmaus. What else would he expect? Perhaps the disciples sat in stunned silence and awe for a while; however, eventually they would need to "come out of it." He who knew all things could have done nothing but expect his disciples to talk with each other, to marvel together, to ask each other for corroboration that all this was not a dream.

This time, Jesus needed to issue no invitation to respond, as he had done on the road. He sent forth his Spirit deep within them to guide their discussion. And what a discussion it must have been! We know little of what was actually said; we only know of their recognition of why they were so stirred on the journey.

What Luke reports of that discussion is not a statement but a question, "Were not our hearts burning?" I think that because they ask themselves this question, the disciples were saying, "We should have known. The signs were there." Perhaps they berated themselves a little for their inability to recognize him, or maybe they could finally laugh at them-

---

3   Buisson, "Le Christ," 72.

selves as no doubt Jesus had. "We really were deadheads, weren't we?"

This time of discussion was like a debriefing, and good teachers encourage it at the end of a course. It's a transition point that allows the students to look backward and forward at the same time. They are still in the safety area of the classroom, although their minds and hearts are partially out the door. The discussion of what each individual has experienced creates a sense of what "we as a group" feel about it and what we will do next.

Sometimes we teachers request a formal evaluation of the course by the students, but that is not mutual discussion. Perhaps the best way to carry out this debriefing is for us to leave the room, as Jesus did, leaving some questions to the students such as,

- What did you learn?

- What did you get out of the course?

- What will you remember most, and why?

- What will you do with it?

- What will it cost you to act?

It takes a pretty secure teacher to let this discussion take place, but there at Emmaus is our model. If the teacher has followed the Emmaus catechetical approach, it is no longer a question of whether to accept the information but how to use it.

We know the disciples spent little time in this discussion, because Luke next says they "got up immediately."

Before we move on to what they did then, I would like to suggest, along with Buisson, that we catechists engage in discussion ourselves, just as the disciples did after the Eucharist. We all too often isolate ourselves in our work, or we feel we are alone; yet the truth is, we do not search alone but with others who are asking the same questions. We too are students, and our subject is how to teach. That is why teamwork is so important when it comes to educating students, particularly those in the early stages of human development.

10. They Got Up Immediately and Returned to Jerusalem

*I*nterestingly, and very importantly, the Emmaus story ends with neither the eucharistic meal nor the discussion between the disciples in the same room where the Eucharist had taken place, as Buisson notes about this final stage. The disciples hurried back to Jerusalem, back to their original departure point. The final point of their journey turned out to be where it had begun. They went nearly full circle—except, of course, that they were no longer at the same starting point, spiritually and even emotionally, as when they had begun.

The Emmaus road mirrored this imagery. From Jerusalem to Emmaus, the road led downhill. The road back was thus uphill. But on the wings of their newly vindicated faith, the hardship must have seemed minor to the disciples. Surely the more difficult of the two journeys had been the earlier one.

As Soeur Jeanne d'Arc explains this last step of Emmaus:

> When we are impregnated by this light of
> Christ, transformed by this contact, our hearts
> catch fire and from them flows charitable,
> loving, divine action: Go and do likewise. When
> the Word has nourished us, when grace has
> refreshed us by means of water and wine, oil
> and bread, when the Spirit has sent us a servant,
> when we have encountered Christ on the way, it
> is then we go to our brothers. We take up our
> journey in joy once more, as did the eunuch
> [who while traveling by carriage had been
> seeking the meaning of Scripture—Acts 8,
> 26-40].[1]

Gillièron describes a similar scenario among the disciples
and, by extension, in later times as well:

> They go get their brothers and take their place
> in the community despite their constant desire
> to flee. They set out to distribute bread to the
> poor despite their meager resources. They
> believe themselves capable of proclaiming the
> Word confidently despite resistance and
> frequent refusal.
> For it is to this that the Lord's meal always
> leads, at Emmaus and elsewhere: a triple
> mission, a triple vocation. We cannot just leave
> the Lord's table as if it were of slight
> consequence.
> But there at least—the point of arrival from
> our wearisome journeys, the point of departure
> for our triple mission—we recognize the Lord.
> And we will recognize Him yet again.[2]

This final scene of Emmaus underscores the fact that
when Christians enter a personal relationship with Christ,

---

[1] Jeanne d'Arc, *Les Pélerins d'Emmaüs*, 205.

[2] Gillièron, *Le Repas d'Emmaüs*, 69.

faith cannot remain individualistic or stay enclosed within a small, close-knit group. Our faith must go beyond; it must bring others into the believing community or, if they are already in it, bring them to the fullness of revelation. The disciples had to return to tell the others what they could still scarcely believe had happened to them. Fulfilled faith puts people on the road because of their urge to share the Good News that they cannot keep to themselves.[3]

What will the others find who are brought to the Church by Christians eager to share their faith, Buisson asks. Unfortunately, for some, often (but not only) the young, it is difficult to see in the visible Church the mystery and the sacrament of Christ. They cannot recognize the Church, unless, like the disciples of Emmaus, they catch a glimpse of Jesus alive in it. Then, when he disappears, when they can see him no longer, they will go to the Church, which continually speaks of him and presents him under the form of bread and wine.[4]

As a teacher, I have watched in joy many times when students—mine or those of other teachers—do just as the Emmaus disciples did as they go out to bring others to the Church. I often think we catechists should encourage our students to tell the Good News and invite others to the Church more than we do, but a faith-filled heart thinks to do it naturally and without invitation. If we have done our job well, we probably shouldn't have to encourage such invitations from our students in the first place: they will flow as a matter of course.

I wonder how clearly we catechists realize that when the students' faith is fulfilled, at that point they become teachers. Sometimes it seems all we really expect of them is to live a good individual life, not necessarily to hasten out eagerly,

---

3 Buisson, "Le Christ," 70.

4 Ibid., 72.

like the disciples, to share their faith. We are content if our students attend church and support their parish, marry and raise children according to Church norms. Raising little Christians obviously requires that parents do some teaching, yet they often say they don't know how and turn over the job to teachers, who in turn say they need the parents' help. If the parents have never shared their faith with others, how can they do it with their children?

Keeping the final stage of the Emmaus journey in mind gives me a higher objective than the typical lesson plan or course goal, and yet it is one I cannot make happen any more than Jesus could. If this final stage of the Emmaus pedagogy belongs not to the teacher but to the student, how, then, do I work on a practical level with it? I can prepare for it by doing my part in the earlier stages, where I am needed as a teacher in different ways at different points on the road. I can also add my own faith in the Master Teacher, my hope and prayer that my students are caught in the same passionate desire as the disciples to tell others what they have learned by experiencing the Lord, not just knowing about him.

When and if I get to see this happening, I can feel I might have succeeded in some small way to teach as Jesus did. But I must always be aware that I may never get to see it, since it may not happen till my students are long gone. The measure of my success may be simply my ongoing faith that it could happen in the first place. That is what keeps me on the road.

Aware of who we are and what our mission is, we make the initial approach; we walk along with the students; we ask them a question; we explain what they need based on what we learn from them; we wait for their response; we celebrate liturgy together; they speak with each other; they get up immediately and return to others to share the good news.

We have traced the Emmaus events and looked at their implications for religious instruction, and we have considered it as a model for meeting the need for re-evangelization in today's world. Let us now move on to Part Three to see, first, the relationship of our catechetical work to the "life journey" or road of development, and, second, some ways to engage our students on their own road toward Emmaus.

Part Three

Teaching through Liturgy

The Catechist As Pilgrim

T he liturgy of the Emmaus journey began as soon as Jesus walked with his disciples. It concluded when the two disciples returned, without fear, to Jerusalem to share their "Good News." The key, then, to living a liturgical life is to walk with Jesus first.

It is important for us teachers to consider that, like our students, we travel along our own road of life as members of the human race. Our first role is that of humans in development; we, too, are learning. When we understand the implications of our own pilgrimage, I think we will be better teachers; for we are then aware of our continual need to learn and practice just as our students must do, and thus we can apply the Emmaus principles more fully.

Because education is such a lengthy process, students (particularly the more serious ones) from time immemorial have been described as setting out on their quest for knowledge. Mayer, for example, portrays the educated person as a tireless traveler always in search of what lies beyond the existing frontiers. He goes on to depict teachers as ever on a pilgrimage in wisdom and knowledge.[1] Ideally, both teacher and student are always seeking new vistas.[2]

Westerhoff has noted the connection of both student and teacher alike to pilgrimage. "To be a catechumen," he comments, "is to be a pilgrim," and "to catechize is to participate with others in the life-long pilgrimage of catechesis...a compassionate companion and guide to pilgrims."[3]

He contrasts this sort of instructor with teachers who are excellent technicians but not true guides. Guides know that they have not yet arrived and that they do not have all the answers, yet they are able to help the fellow pilgrim along the road.[4]

The pilgrim differs from the tourist in that the pilgrim has a particular place in mind, one worthy of special affection and reverence as well as whatever effort is entailed to get there. The road to that point is of interest, but only secondarily. Upon reaching the destination, the pilgrim engages in quiet but joyful contemplation. By contrast, the tourist is a sightseer, following whatever sideroads and attractions may present themselves, one perhaps as good as another.

Pilgrimage in Life and Learning

Life, like education, is a journey, in which we pass from one point to another. Both life and education have long been recognized in this way, and metaphorical imagery abounds.

---

1 Mayer, *Education for Creative Living*, 73, 18.

2 Cf. Koberg and Bagnall, whose *All-New Universal Traveler* develops this theme.

3 Westerhoff and Edwards, *Faithful Church*, 3.

4 Ibid., 302.

For those who are more reflective, the growing and maturing process is easy to think of as a journey, though far more difficult if a destination is not clear or viewed as attainable. The journey theme occurs often in the work of psychologists and educators alike. On a typical journey, every person encounters different stages, and each stage entails unique concerns for those passing through. Thus people need different tactics to help themselves cross to the next stage. However, there is often no precise marker between passages; it is not always possible to tell when the exact point is reached. Nor is the attainment always noted or celebrated, especially in Western culture. Yet enormous interest in the metaphor of the journey through life and learning has arisen in the developmental psychology of Jung, Piaget, Bruner and others, and more recent popularized versions thereof.[5]

These developmental stages—however many a particular framework may list—can be equated with the "life cycle," which Losoncy defines as:

> [A] path which each person follows at his or her
> own pace. No two are exactly the same, yet
> most human beings travel through the...stages
> from pre-natal to death. Each stage of the cycle
> brings with it a unique viewpoint; each stage
> gives us a special vantage point from which to
> view life.[6]

---

[5] Cf. Carl G. Jung, "The Stages of Life," *Modern Man in Search of a Soul* (New York: Harcourt, 1933); Hans G. Furth, *Piaget and Knowledge: Theoretical Foundations* (Englewood Cliffs, New Jersey: Prentice-Hall Inc., 1969); Jerome Bruner, *Toward a Theory of Instruction* (New York: W. W. Norton & Company, Inc., 1966); Erik Erikson, *Childhood and Society*, rev. ed. (New York: Norton, 1963); Gail Sheehy, *Passages: Predictable Crises of Adult Life* (New York: Dutton, 1976): Janet Hagbert and Richard Leider, *The Inventures: Excursions in Life and Career Renewal*, rev. ed. (Reading, Massachusetts: Addison-Wesley Publishing Company, 1982).

[6] Losoncy, *Religious Education and the Life Cycle*, 3.

Successful passage through the stages of human development assists successful passage through the stages of education. Catechesis has increasingly considered the importance of understanding human development. Maves, for instance, comments that the religious dimension as an experiential dimension or behavior response is related to the total personality structure; thus, changes in religious belief, attitudes, and behavior are influenced by the conditions determining changes in any other area of human life.[7] So too Kohlberg has broken ground in showing how moral development is linked to the developmental stages,[8] and others have looked at the development of religious thinking in youth.[9] Jorgensen has made an excellent diagrammatic linkage between a number of the developmental psychological theories, showing the interrelation of the various life periods each proposes.[10]

As teachers, being aware of our own personal journey is an important aspect of our own development, let alone of assisting in the development of our students. When we acknowledge that we are still journeying, we are more likely to become what Knowles calls "lifetime learners"[11] and thus be more ready to engage in conscious pilgrimage in the Church.

---

[7] Maves, "Religious Development," 783.

[8] Kohlberg and Turiel, *Recent Research in Moral Judgment*; Kohlberg, "Revisions in the Theory and Practice of Moral Development," 83-88.

[9] Cf. Fowler, *Stages of Faith*; Goldman, *Religious Thinking from Childhood to Adolescence*.

[10] Jorgensen, *Rekindling the Passion*, 221-227.

[11] This term is introduced and developed in Knowles' *Adult Learner*.

Pilgrimage in the Church

The Church's entire calling is that of pilgrimage:

> The church is a pilgrim community of memory
> and vision. The vocation of the church is to hear
> God speak, to see God act, and to witness in
> word and deed to these experiences.
> Christianity from the beginning has been
> essentially a missionary community: the Gospel
> has been committed to the community.[12]

Vatican II used much metaphor and imagery of the pilgrim to apply to the Church, rediscovering her very roots in the wandering people of the old covenant:

> As Israel according to the flesh which wandered
> in the desert was already called the Church of
> God (2 Esd 13:1; cf. Num. 20:4: Deut. 23:1ff.), so
> too, the new Israel, which advances in this
> present era in search of a future and permanent
> city (cf. Heb. 13:14), is called also the Church of
> Christ (cf. Mt. 16:18)....Advancing through trials
> and tribulations, the Church is strengthened by
> God's grace....[13]

Thus the Church is "like a stranger in a foreign land, pressing forward amid the persecutions of the world and the consolations of God," with a mission of announcing the cross and death of Jesus until he comes again.[14]

The pilgrim imagery expresses the communion of saints, a "union of wayfarers," some still traveling on earth, some being purified, and some already in glory.[15]

---

[12] Fuchs, "Task of the Religious Educator," 4.

[13] "Dogmatic Constitution on the Church" ("Lumen Gentium"), *Vatican Council II: The Conciliar and Post-Conciliar Documents*, n.9.

[14] Ibid., n.8.

[15] Ibid., n.49.

> In full consciousness of this communion of the
> whole Mystical Body of Jesus Christ, the Church
> in its pilgrim members, from the very earliest
> days of the Christian religion, has honored with
> great respect the memory of the dead....Exactly
> as Christian communion between men on their
> earthly pilgrimage brings us closer to Christ, so
> our community with the saints joins us to
> Christ, as from its fountain and head issues all
> grace and the life of the People of God itself.[16]

Mary, mother of Jesus, is honored as a fellow wayfarer
whose own pilgrimage is worthy of particular respect and
honor. Vatican II looked upon her as the "sign of certain hope
and comfort to the pilgrim people of God."[17] Pope John Paul
II took up this theme:

> Strengthened by the presence of Christ (cf. Mt.
> 28:20), the Church journeys through time
> towards the consummation of the ages and goes
> to meet the Lord who comes. But on this
> journey...she proceeds along the path already
> trodden by the Virgin Mary, who "advanced in
> her pilgrimage of faith and loyally persevered in
> her union with her Son unto the cross."[18]

This excerpt introduces one of his main themes in
Redemptoris Mater: Mary has already made the faith pilgrimage, blessed because she believed, as Elizabeth described her
when she traveled to her home upon learning of her mirac-
ulous pregnancy.[19]

I wish to consider primarily that "pilgrimage of faith" in
which the Blessed Virgin "advanced," faithfully preserving

---

[16] "Dogmatic Constitution on the Church" ("Lumen Gentium"),
Vatican Council II: The Conciliar and Post-Conciliar Documents, n.50.

[17] Ibid., n.68.

[18] John Paul II, "Mother of the Redeemer" ("Redemptoris Mater"), n.2.

[19] Ibid., n.5.

her union with Christ. In this way the bond which unites the mother of God with Christ and with the Church takes on historical significance. It is not just a question of the Virgin Mother's life story, of her personal journey of faith, and the choice blessing which is hers in the mystery of salvation; it is also a question of the history of the whole people of God, of all those who take part in the same "pilgrimage of faith."

Mary continues to precede us on the way to Christ in a historical journey:

> The pilgrimage of faith indicates the interior history, that is, the story of souls. Here...the Blessed Virgin Mary continues "to go before" the People of God. Her exceptional pilgrimage of faith represents a constant point of reference for the Church, for individuals and for communities, for peoples and nations and, in a sense, for all humanity.[20]

The Church, then:

> [F]rom the beginning has modelled her earthly journey on that of the Mother of God [and] constantly repeats after her the words of the Magnificat.[21]

For those on the Church's pilgrimage, the imagery of Cyril and his catechumens exploring the Holy City in mystagogical catechesis come to mind: the world becomes a New Jerusalem from which to learn of Jesus. For teachers who are aware of themselves as engaged on this pilgrimage, their true status is clear: they are fellow journeyers with their students, both of whom the Master Teacher approaches on the road to invite to his eucharistic meal.

---

[20] John Paul II, "Mother of the Redeemer" ("Redemptoris Mater"), n.2.
[21] Ibid., n.37.

On the Road: Toward Liturgy

*L*et us see now how the journeying teacher can help the journeying students on their way. First let us view the Emmaus principles translated for the catechist:

1. Jesus knew himself—what his identity was, who he was.

2. Jesus knew his mission—what he was about.

3. Jesus approached the disciples in person.

4. Jesus walked along with them.

5. He said to them, "What are you discussing as you go your way?"

6. Then he said to them, "O foolish [dear witless] ones, slow to believe all that the prophets foretold!"

7. He made as if to go further.

8. Once at the table, he took bread, blessed it, broke it, and gave it to them, whereupon their eyes were opened and they recognized him.

9. They spoke with each other.

10. They got up immediately and returned to Jerusalem.

During the first part of the Emmaus catechetical approach, the catechist consciously makes an effort to meet students where they are. This is not quite the same as, say, a teacher of a secular subject who simply uses individualized lesson plans or learning styles to meet students where they are. These can and should be used in any pedagogy. But used alone, without the liturgical element, they would not complete the Emmaus pedagogy, in which catechists are aware that they are going to travel together with the students toward the eucharistic meal.

From the beginning, then, liturgy colors the thinking and planning of the catechist, just as it will eventually color the catechetical content as well, just as Jesus at the outset of the Emmaus journey knew what he was going to do at the end of the road if the disciples went that far with him.

It is enough that the catechist, irrespective of subject matter, look for ways to meet the student on the road. In this way, the Emmaus pedagogy can be applied to even a non-religious subject, with the notion that further down the road—and with continual prayer for the students—the catechist will look for ways to guide their students' steps toward the meeting with Jesus. Depending on the circumstances, this meeting may be one in which Jesus is met less immediately and less directly than in the Eucharist; however, the students will experience Jesus' real presence through the catechist's own close walk with him. The catechist can offer each teaching moment, each encounter with the students, "in remembrance of me," of Jesus. Obviously, the Emmaus approach is more difficult to apply in more secular settings.

Let us now look at how the Emmaus approach could be applied in a catechetical situation.

Steps 1 and 2 Prior to the course, the catechist takes stock of his or her identity and mission, best done in prayer and liturgy.

Step 3 The catechist approaches the students, sharing something of himself or herself.

Step 4 The catechist carries out an initial discussion of the course and how it fits into the larger picture, going into various details necessary to get underway.

Step 5 The catechist raises questions which can in part be done as activities beyond the confines of the classroom. Here the catechist can find out a bit about the students' personal knowledge of Jesus—not so much facts (although the students' factual knowledge should be ascertained also) but more about how they relate to him. The following are some activities to discover this:

Activity: Students discuss or write about who Jesus is and how they find him relevant—if at all—in the lives of others and in their lives (that order is somewhat easier for students to deal with). Discussion starters can include:

- Whom do they know who seems to know Jesus? What are the clues that indicate this person's relationship with him?

- How do they know when Jesus is relevant to them?

- What is most difficult about personally following Jesus? What is easiest? Why?

Activity: Paraphrase Gospel stories or well-chosen spiritual writings.

Activity: Write self-evaluations which ad-dress the extent to which Jesus' relevance is important to the students directly rather than to family or friends.

Activity: Students provide the teacher with information about their grasp of the subject as well as its relevance for them personally.

Step 6 The catechist now engages in prayerful reflection—not just "teacher planning"—asking the Lord's help in this endeavor. On the basis of what the teacher has learned about the students, if basic evangelization seems needed that should now be planned for in the course. Remember that to try to carry out a full-scale catechetical course when basic evangelization is needed—even if there is a mandate to cover certain catechetical points— would be the total opposite of how the Lord himself proceeded. The teaching can be understood so much better by students when they have truly received the Good News.

Although students will always be at various faith levels (just as their physical, intellectual, and spiritual development will vary), the teacher will likely detect a general "tone" in the group, which will indicate how to proceed. The catechist may want to assign those students at higher levels to work on special projects together, or individually depending on need, so that evangelization may take place more easily.

Of course, evangelization may be carried out in any of a number of ways; but the catechist can take a cue from the way Jesus used stories from which he could draw out other points when he was first spreading his message.

Step 7   The catechist leads to a place where an invitation can be issued to the students to go further, even if they are still within the time of evangelization. In this way, students will feel they are being treated as the responsible persons they must eventually grow to be.

How does the catechist know when the moment has come to issue the invitation? The teacher will not only feel a general comfort level but also will start to receive feedback from students as they begin to open up in class or outside on a experiential level. The catechist should strive for this level of sharing personal insights and dialoguing, rather than staying at the level of dispensing factual knowledge and allowing students to speak only when called on.

What form should the invitation take? It depends. This is something to start thinking about back in the fifth and sixth steps. How will the catechist know? Let the Spirit lead.

Step 8   It might be time for a real liturgy, which will be discussed later, or perhaps an informal prayer service, which can be a point of departure as to how liturgy is ongoing prayer and service in daily life.

Step 9   It might simply be time for some deeper sharing than has occurred so far. Perhaps it will be commitment and action selected by the students. These are all presences of the Lord and thus, to an extent, "meals" with him.

131

In any event, it is possible and desirable to build in some appreciation of the liturgy as a particular, even prime, place to encounter Jesus. The Emmaus story itself could be an excellent point of departure. Perhaps the class can enjoy a laugh as they realize the situation is about a teacher and dense students; perhaps they can gain appreciation of how good Jesus in the role of the teacher was. What can they find in the story that pertains to their own experience in learning religious or other subjects?

Step 10 This is the step that is up to the students. Hopefully, they will want to go share and, in so doing, be a more integral part of the community. Perhaps the catechist could gently encourage the students to consider what they wish to do next.

Activities for Linking the Liturgy to the Journey

To tie the liturgy into the journey, some activities may be assigned to students of all ages in a religious course to prepare the way for greater participation later in the liturgy. Such activities could include, but are not limited to, the following.

Understanding Symbols

Because so many people today, particularly in modern society, have lost their appreciation for ritual and symbolism, it would seem a good idea to develop that sense all over again in order to foster liturgical life. It might be worthwhile to name some rituals and symbols to see just how, even today, they are important.

Obviously, ritual and symbolism are alive and well in the sports world, to mention but one modern area. Native American symbolism, long integrated into youth programs, has fascinated young people, who often adopt their own symbols and names. Then too, there are the family or individual rituals, ranging from how the family celebrates ("We must have Grandma's pearl onions or it's not Thanksgiving") to individual ones ("I must wear the red plaid shirt to take the test").

Fuchs suggests a sequential program for religious educators to help students develop an appreciation for symbols, starting with the existing symbols of their faith and moving "from the inside outward." His plan goes outside the liturgy itself, but not very far.[1]

1. Sensitize students to the language of the symbolic so that they can approach the symbolic dimension. Let them look at and discuss real or depicted symbols. They must handle the symbols with care, letting them speak, fostering their particular language, allowing them to be neither overexplained or negated.

2. Help students critique the forms and uses of the symbolic that might misuse or delimit its power.

3. Help students become aware of the various experiences of human life in general as well as those of the body and the environment and the poetic imagination to catch hints of the symbolic that lie dormant, for they may find new

---

[1] Fuchs, "Task of the Religious Educator," 2.

symbols to empower them for the journey
on which they now travel.

4. Provide the student with critical,
interpretive tools by which to recover or
reclaim the symbols of his or her tradition.
Having students make up their own
symbols and rituals is something they can
really get into. Even adults gain from it, as
many retreat participants can attest.

Understanding Various Types of Journeys

Students can also work with insights from developmental psychology and imagery, such as the Maronite portrayal of the road to the kingdom as birth from three wombs—from the mother, at baptism, and at death—as well as the spring emerging from winter and the cocoon becoming the butterfly. This imagery can be woven into any religious course; in fact, the latter can be woven into secular courses as undergirding for the notion of the celebration of rebirth.

The ancient pilgrim imagery, rediscovered in Vatican II, including Mary as pilgrim prototype of us all, is adaptable for all age levels. Similarly, it is possible to draw from authors over the centuries who have written of the spiritual journey.

The study of wandering peoples (nomads, gypsies, Jews and Christians in diaspora) as well as the significance of pilgrimages in history, the difference between a "pilgrim" and a "tourist"—all can be excellent topics which help students gain perspective on their personal journeys. For students who have immigrated from other countries, studying pilgrim imagery can be very meaningful in helping them express their feelings and by giving them a model for their new experience.

The mystagogical catechesis of Cyril of Jerusalem might serve as a model for learning as pilgrims. The class may want to study sites where Jesus walked and taught, through judicious use of pictures and videotapes, if not real travel.

Understanding Liturgical Dimensions of Life

How can the catechist help students grasp the liturgical dimensions of life? Surely one of the best ways for the catechist to start is to live more liturgically, not just attending liturgies for his or her own benefit but for the students' benefit as well. Above all, the Emmaus pedagogy entails the catechist's being comfortable with—and loving!—liturgical living.

The catechist can become conscious of the fact that he or she is part of an ongoing liturgy: the heavenly and earthly liturgy in unison. If the catechist does this ever more consciously, he or she can pass on this awareness. Only if the catechist is fully part of the family can he or she welcome new members into it.

This work entails recalling and reconstructing Christ's message so that it becomes conscious and active in one's individual and community life. In this regard, the catechist may well need to expand his or her view of what liturgy is. People often think of liturgy as just the service on Sunday, but real liturgical living takes people into the ongoing life of Jesus in a sequence of the most important events he lived. *Any* liturgy brings the faithful into his presence, but a *particular* liturgy celebrating one of those events in the framework of the liturgical year brings him and his followers together at that point in his life. In this way, "understanding liturgical dimensions of life" flows directly into "living them."

Some points the catechist could try to recall frequently and help the students grasp are these:

- The liturgy itself allows the faithful not only to look backward historically but forward eschatologically, thus climbing to a high point from which to view and live life—above the flat humdrum world in which it is so easy to get entrapped.

Activity: Students could either go up a hill for an excursion or just look at pictures taken from a high vantage point and discuss how the perspective on life's ordinary view seems from that point. Then the views can be linked with the view provided within the liturgy.

- By living liturgically, the catechist is walking on a road that is much more than his or her own: it is Jesus Christ's. Walking Jesus' road with the Church moves the traveler from a straight road to a circular one, or a spiral, for it passes through the events of Jesus' life one by one on a yearly basis.

Activity: Students could draw or discuss pictures of a straight road and a spiral (curving upward) road, marking each with personal events and events from the life of Jesus. Then compare the two types to see which they find more helpful and accurate from them.

- Another dimension that liberates the traveler from the confines of his or her own narrow road is the convergence of the human with the divine. How does this convergence occur? The events of Jesus' life are the same; he has lived them. But as we *celebrate* them in the seasons of the liturgical year, our own lives are still unfolding. So as we

approach Christmas or Easter or any
other feast, we celebrate differently
because every passing year is never quite
the same; we are in different stages of
development. Too, the outside world and
the Church are also in different stages of
development. For those who realize this,
the liturgical and secular calendar
become blended.

Activity: Students could be encouraged to create
their own liturgical and life calendars. They could
make symbols or color the dates of birthdays, grad-
uations, and other family events as well as holy
days. They could refer to their calendars throughout the year in class, interrelating their own lives
with that of Jesus. They could discuss their own
development and their new insights at various
points in the year.

• The liturgical event, by being always
new, provides new opportunities to learn
and is thus a way in which Jesus can
reinforce his teaching, as when he
walked the earth:

> He was not done with a lesson when
> he had taught it, or with a class when
> he had addressed it. Teaching was
> too big a thing to be over with so
> soon. In his conception it is a life
> process and is not finished until life
> is perfected. So we find him adopting
> measures to reinforce what we may
> call his classroom instruction and
> translate it into faith and character.[2]

---

2 Marquis, *Learning to Teach*, 34.

137

Nor is Jesus finished even today with his teaching, if the faithful let him continue through his real presence in the liturgy—year in, year out. If education could be called a "feast of knowledge," the liturgy is that feast and more, because it is experiential rather than simply intellectual knowledge and can thus take the followers of Jesus further up the educational taxonomy.

> Mass is no time for theologizing, for class, for moving the mind....It is time for liberating the soul. Time for communion.[3]

Activity: Students could be encouraged to reflect on how participation in liturgy can be a source of healing and unifying their minds to grasp spiritual and temporal truths more readily. They could also share new insights about the liturgy from time to time.

- Although the challenge of the liturgy is to make it "come alive," its experiential dimension is limitless, as Shea points out in his introduction to Karl Rahner's *The Eternal Year*:

> In the Eucharist the Church possesses the total, living Christ of the present, the risen Lord with his eternal sacrifice, his eternal priesthood, his eternal victimhood. The risen life that he now lives, obtained through his death, he pours out upon us most fully through the Eucharist, the sun and center of the

---

[3] O'Malley, "Toward an Adult Spirituality," 344.

sacramental world. Here is the
source of all life, here is the
sacrament that unifies all else. But we
are still limited by the time and space
of earthly flesh. We cannot think of
or experience everything at once; so
we cannot appreciate the Eucharist
all at once. For our sakes the one
single vivifying reality, compressed
and concentrated in the Eucharist, is
broken down through the Church's
liturgical year. God does not need
feasts and seasons; we do.[4]

Activity: This need of ours, rather than God's, for feasts and seasons could be a discussion topic of great value.

- As the traveler appreciates the seasons of nature, so too the teacher needs to live in accord with the seasons of the liturgy. Some Christian cultures are so imbued with this liturgical sense that people think of the secular season in terms of the religious one. Maronite Christians, for instance, still often refer to particular days not so much as dates but as religious feasts, saying, for instance, "Good weather disappears after the Feast of the Cross."

Activity: Discussion could be very productive about life amid seasons, both natural and liturgical—or what the consequences are without them.

- The liturgy can be regarded as a source of light. The Church year, in which liturgical activity takes place, is like the

---

4   Shea, Introduction to Rahner, *Eternal Year*, 9.

cathedrals of the Middle Ages, which were educational treasuries with their resplendent stained-glass windows. The liturgy also refracts the light, but unlike them, it is living. It is as if one strong dazzling beam of light shone down upon us from the risen Lord; this beam is refracted and diffused for our weak eyes through the spectrum of the Church year. Just as we cannot see the richness of the colors contained in a single beam of sunlight unless it is sent through a prism, so too the Church year shows us all the different aspects, all the richness and glory of the one, central, all-embracing, unifying event of the Lord's death and resurrection, which we call the paschal mystery and which we celebrate in the Eucharist.

For this reason the Church has her different seasons, her variety of feasts. For this reason she celebrates the death and resurrection of the Lord in so many different ways: at Easter and in Holy Week; in the Ascension and at Pentecost; at Christmas and Epiphany; in Advent and Lent; in other feasts of the Lord, his mother, and his saints. The Church year is a precious diamond in the hands of our mother the Church; slowly she turns it around so that we may see every facet, every aspect of it. It is one stone (Easter) with many facets (all the feasts).[5]

Activity: Students might be given colored glass or rock crystals and encouraged to share insights on

---

[5] Shea, Introduction to Rahner, *Eternal Year*, 10.

the refracted light. Discussion could tie those insights to what the liturgy does in refracting the divine light.

• To live liturgically requires admission that the One who comes in that liturgy is needed:

> Christ came for the sick, but most of us claim to be healthy. Or at least OK. Until we admit our need, we will never admit our dependence, and until we admit our dependence we will never seek the only food to feed the deepest part of ourselves— not only the Eucharist but the "freshest deep-down things," who is everywhere we turn, if only we had eyes sensitized to see and ears sensitized to hear. Even in a "boring" Mass. In impoverishing our own spirits, we impoverish the spirits of our children.[6]

Activity: Students could be encouraged to discuss various areas where they sense a need for Jesus to come to them to help them or others. Or they could discuss where in a liturgy they felt his presence.

• Liturgical living is not confined to celebrating inside a building. Pious Jews, living in the spirit of their own liturgy, actually have a rabbinic tradition obliging them to offer praise and thanksgiving to the Lord Creator when they come across one of the miracles in His creation (*qiddush levanah*).[7] This way

---

[6] O'Malley, "Toward an Adult Spirituality," 344.

[7] Klein, *Guide to Jewish Religious Practice,* 267.

of being open to the altar of creation is similar to what Rochelle means by saying liturgy is an attitude, an approach to life.[8]

How important that teachers become—and help their students become—liturgical people, for then all can be taught by Jesus on the road wherever they may be. A teacher will remember more easily that Jesus loves to do this; in turn he or she can help the students remember it, too, and appreciate the way Jesus does so anywhere and everywhere. Marquis remarks on Jesus' "wayside teaching":

> In the Master's view there are no wayside incidents in life, in the sense that they are trifling or unimportant. Everything that happens is important and purposeful.[9]

Activities to help students grasp *qiddush levanah* in everyday life include:

Activity: Take or send the students on an excursion to notice as if for the first time things in the neighborhood that reflect God's hand. Give thanks for these insights.

Activity: Make the Stations of the Cross while walking through the neighborhood to share in atoning for those areas of life where all is not at peace.

Activity: Keep journals of blessings and answered prayers, then share some of them with others.

---

8 Rochelle, *Revolutionary Year*, 1.

9 Marquis, *Learning to Teach*, 40.

Activity: Reliving the Emmaus events themselves could be a point of departure. For example, a retreat could be conducted with small groups in which the leader and participants represent Jesus and the disciples. Go on a seven-mile walk, reenacting the events of Luke's story. Roles could be interchanged. At journey's end, celebrate a liturgy. Participants would not only discuss but also go share Jesus with others.

Celebrating an Actual Liturgy

In catechesis, making liturgy a point of departure can be done in several ways, although it is best done as part of an ongoing, systematic program, not as isolated segments of lessons here and there. Here are several possibilities.

Liturgy Celebrated to Mark Milestones

Liturgical rites may be celebrated as milestones to mark various points along the students' journeys, whether church-related or more generally life-related. Because the liturgy would celebrate milestones along what is recognized as a journey, such as the entry into faith, it would provide an ideal educational opportunity for it can express and focus on the journey up to that point as well as beyond. For example, with regard to the *Rite of Christian Initiation for Adults*, Kelly points out:

> Its various stages signal that, for Catholics,
> conversion is usually a gradual, step-by-step
> process, and not the Protestant evangelistic,
> once-in-a-lifetime, "born-again" experience.
> Liturgical rites used at the various stages of the
> process remind us of how heart, spirit and mind
> are all involved in the initiation process. All

these dimensions are also needed in the catechetical process that accompanies and deepens initiation.[10]

If certain sacraments are understood as the true rites of passage that they are, and are added to other life stages as well, adapting a scheme of Westerhoff[11] provides a good guide for the point at which liturgical-catechetical activity is particularly appropriate:

Non-Sacramental	Sacramental
Birth/Adoption of a Child	Baptism (joined with Confirmation/Chrismation in Eastern churches)
	First Communion
Responsibility	Confirmation (in Western churches)
Life in Christian Community	
Commitment of Christian Service	

These last three stages in life might be a good time for liturgical celebrations of passage along the lines of the Jewish *bar* or *bat mitzvah*, the point when a young man or woman confronts the freedom of impending adulthood with its parallel obligations.

Liturgies in the home may be an especially helpful way to recall the original Christian liturgies as well as to mark milestones along an individual Christian's life road. While getting a priest may not always be easy in certain localities, it is an idea that, with advance planning, is so memorable as to be well worth any difficulty. In the absence of a priest and an official liturgy, a simple prayerful commemoration designed around the event—while never the same as a lit-

---

[10] Kelly, "Catechetical Journey," 224.

[11] Westerhoff and Edwards, *Faithful Church*, 312-314.

urgy—can also serve to communally mark the occasion in the life of the Church extended.

The catechist has a wonderful role to carry out in showing concern and love for students by helping them design and by participating with them in particular liturgies as well as regular liturgies. The catechist's participation is a beautiful symbol of affirmation of the joint pilgrim status both catechist and student share. Leading students directly to the liturgy can be the point at which the catechist has most completely fulfilled the instructional role. The catechist may choose to share that feeling of fulfillment with the students; except by open testimony, perhaps the students might never otherwise be aware of the catechist's personal appreciation of his or her role.

Understanding the Liturgical Year

Clearly this understanding can be fostered through homilies and parish bulletin handouts. The homily, however, often focuses on just the feast of the day rather than how it fits into a whole season and how that season fits into the entire liturgical year. The homily could also help focus on where the events of the Gospel reading of the day fit into in the life of Jesus.

Just as homilies and parish bulletin handouts should foster understanding of where a specific feast fits into the overall Church year, so too should they help people understand how ritual and symbols fit into the liturgy.

However, for best results, more instruction is needed than during the actual liturgy. Without understanding ritual and symbols, a whole dimension is lost to many. Perhaps an occasional mention of some of the things converts say about this would be a motivator within the parish, let alone a religion class. It could be still more effective to invite the converts to give their personal testimonies to the students.

Involving more people in the parish—not just a liturgy committee or clergy—in planning and implementing liturgies is energizing to the life of the parish as well as to those who do the planning. People are often reticent to try, but if given one small part of the total effort, especially if part of a team, they will often surprise even themselves. Small successes foster larger efforts.

Other Liturgies and Liturgically Related Prayer

The Angelus, a short adaptation of the Liturgy of the Hours (Divine Office), with the marking off of the times of the day, and the rosary, with its marking off the mysteries of salvation, and of course the full-scale version of the Liturgy of the Hours are excellent ways of fostering a liturgical spirit. However, it will be helpful for the catechist to provide training, teaching, and witnessing to the effectiveness of these pious practices, for many complain that they find these practices boring, or cannot remember to take a break during their busy day.

Living liturgically and engaging in liturgically related exercises are like being in an athletic program. It takes practice, probably with a "team" of others who are committed to doing so also. Those who put these practices into action often say that they assist themselves in better getting into the true rhythm of life and that they become freer from demands of the hectic world, which threaten to overwhelm if nothing is done to resist them. The analogy between athletics and faithfulness in prayer might be a good one to use with young people; they could be invited to try out a program like the Liturgy of the Hours for a while, then share results.

The Liturgy of the Hours is—if understood well—a wonderful spiritual aid, helping us appreciate and use the gift of time all the better:

> In every liturgical action God comes, in his Son, to human beings and sanctifies them by the power of his word that is spoken to us in the Prayer of the Hours (psalms, readings, etc.) no less than in the Mass, but also by the power of the paschal mystery that produces its fruitful effects in encounter and communion with Christ.
>
> Not only is the prayer of the hours characterized by a relationship to the various times of the day; in many of its texts it also proclaims the mystery proper to the seasons and feasts of the liturgical year. Because of its greater length it can develop and meditate on the message of God's saving deeds more fully than is possible in the celebrating of the eucharist.[12]

Familiarity with Other Rites and Faith Liturgies

Within the Catholic Church are a number of rites, not just the Latin. Persons in larger-populated areas often have the opportunity to go to churches where these rites are offered, there to discover the riches of celebrations of feasts shared by both Eastern and Western churches as well as feasts particular to one rite. It is a beautiful experience that too few—primarily in the Western Church—have discovered.

Where this is not possible, programs can be developed (particularly on videotape) that would portray celebration of feasts.

The Christian liturgy draws much from the Jewish liturgy. While it would be desirable to visit synagogues, why

---

[12] Westerhoff, *Pilgrim People*, 308ff.

should we Christians not celebrate the same feasts as well? They are our family inheritance!

Each Catholic parish or school program could do so. In the forefront are an ever-growing number of non-denominational Christian churches whose members are Jews who have accepted Christ. These churches celebrate these feasts, thrilling to the realization of their fulfillment in the Messiah who has already come, while continuing to share the bond with the Jewish family of faith, recalling as do Jews on Passover everywhere that "we were all in bondage in Egypt," even those not born at that time.

Sequenced Instruction About Liturgy

If the liturgy is studied as a subject, it would be desirable to do so on an ongoing basis, whether in Catholic school, the parish at large, or other programs. But the training should not be focused around just one initiative: it should be something that is encouraged for all ages and on a continuing basis. Thus, not just students but parents and all parish staff are encouraged and assisted to develop their knowledge about, appreciation for, and participation in liturgy.

Liturgy is, after all, preparation for life, not just something to be done in the front of the church every Sunday. The catechist needs to help students grasp this, and activities such as I have suggested earlier to prepare students for following Jesus to the Eucharist will help them see how related liturgy is to everyday life.

A central theme of such a course should be the heavenly liturgy at which we all hope to celebrate. If students have responded to the Lord's invitation delivered through their catechist, they will have long ago carried out Emmaus principles 9 and 10, recognizing Jesus in the liturgy and hastening to share the Good News with others; and all will meet, teachers and students alike, to celebrate liturgy forever.

Preparing Catechists

*T*he Emmaus journey we make, whether as teachers or students, in the Christian endeavor, is with Jesus and companions. Elias points out how faith is truly a collective journey:

> Though religious faith can be viewed as an activity in which a person engages, it is better viewed as the personal story of an individual or a religious journey that a person travels with God, self, and others. The story and the journey are difficult ones because their ways, paths, perils, and final destination are not clearly known. One gets the strength to travel the religious journey because of the realization that one does not travel alone. Many millions of religious persons have traveled through this life before, aided by a spiritual vision. Also, persons of faith usually have the support of others in their religious journeys.[1]

---

1   Elias, *Foundations and Practice of Adult Religious Education*, 66.

While I hope liturgy will be used in a deeper way within the religious instructional context, let us recall that Jesus himself did not have much patience with the ritual of the temple if it became off-center. He would not wish liturgy or the teaching associated with it to become routine, because routinization is the danger for the human enterprise. It is an "occupational hazard" and something to keep working against so that those who celebrate liturgy cannot resist going back on the road to invite others. The best way to do this is to be continually on the road with Jesus, continually with our welcoming host at the liturgy, and then to "get up immediately and return to the others" who await him through us. As Corbon says, the liturgy essentially involves action and energy.[2]

In this final chapter, I offer a program for catechists who would like to prepare to engage in the Emmaus pedagogy. This chapter is dedicated to bringing about the proposed catechetical program based on the Emmaus pedagogy. I hope this new pedagogical strategy of lifelong liturgical process according to the Emmaus account will serve as a basis for those willing to take the risk and walk with the Teacher along that fascinating journey.

The starting point at which to learn how to apply the Emmaus pedagogy is obviously the Emmaus events themselves, focusing on how Jesus worked with his disciples at each point. These should be studied by reading and meditating reflectively over a period of time the account of events, Luke 24, 13-35.

A friend of mine in catechesis has continually done so over an entire year and tells me that she has still gained new insights. This is of course what happens when we delve into Scripture: the stories have an incredible way of becoming alive.

---

2   Corbon, *Wellspring of Worship*, 38.

It is not necessary to undergo formal training to use the Emmaus pedagogy to some extent, and even those tangentially associated with religious instruction can do so. This chapter provides a suggested preparation sequence.

For those not yet teaching, this preparation should be very helpful in giving them a pedagogical model that can guide their work from the start. For those already teaching, they can use this exercise to rejuvenate their work.

Preparation for Reflection on the Emmaus Principles

1. Photocopy the ten reflection pages with the Emmaus principles in the appendix. There is a space at the top for you to later fill in the dates when you will focus on that principle.

2. Bring these pages, a New Testament, a looseleaf journal, a pen or pencil, and a calendar along with you for several hours alone and away in a special place and at a special time of peace and quiet, such as by a stream or on a mountain some Sunday afternoon.

3. There, read the Emmaus story in Luke.

4. Make notes in your special "Emmaus journal" of a few insights that seem particularly striking, and why.

5. Mark off ten consecutive periods of time—whether days, weeks, or months—which will be devoted to your Emmaus catechetical study. For example, you may choose ten days (Sunday of

Week 1 through Tuesday of Week 2), ten weeks (April 1 through June 5), or ten months (January through October). If you are part of a team in which this has already been decided and agreed on, this will be an easy matter.

6. If you are planning for a short period of reflection, such as ten days rather than ten weeks, try to plan for a second, longer period of reflection later.

7. Write the dates on each of the ten reflection pages in your journal to mark when you will focus on that particular principle.

8. In planning ahead for the period of reflection on each principle, expect to spend three separate study times of at least fifteen minutes in your quiet place.

9. Coming back from your special place and time, take a long walk—literally—with the Lord as if journeying together. What does he show you and move you to think of as you go? Walk slowly together.

Reflection on the Emmaus Principles

Follow these steps during your ten periods of meditation and prayer on each principle:

1. At the end of each of your meditation and prayer periods, write down an insight in your journal.

2. Periodically share insights on your reflection. If you are not in a formal course, take advantage of friends and family members with whom you can occasionally share insights and ask for their own in turn. Emmaus is a story that everyone enjoys and can respond to.

3. At the end of each of the ten periods, return to your journal to recollect all the insights of that period.

4. Take another walk—literally—with the Lord, thinking over everything you gained during that phase of Emmaus.

5. At the end of your ten periods, work out a lesson plan in light of the Emmaus principles. What will you do, and how will it be different from other lessons you might have taught already, or might teach if you did not prepare in this way? (If you are not yet teaching, simply set up your lesson as if you were going to teach it.)

6. Put the lesson aside for a while, at least for a few days. Plan to attend a liturgy— Sunday or weekday—for which you prepare by asking him to help you feel personally that you are taking part in the Emmaus liturgy. Ask him to share at the liturgy and soon afterward whatever he wishes with you in light of Emmaus.

7. Return to the lesson you wrote. Redo anything you feel moved to change in light of your experience at the liturgy.

I have offered some beginning guidelines in hopes that others will delineate the Emmaus pedagogy still further, for example, in parish or diocesan renewal or large-scale application within catechetical and liturgical endeavors. Toward this end, it is encouraging that not long before the publishing of this study—and totally independent thereof—a catechetics course appeared which made extended reference to the Emmaus events as something that future catechists should consider.[3] I find this an auspicious coincidence.

Although some practical activities have been proposed to help in applying the Emmaus catechetical approach, the purpose of this book remians as sacred and steeped in mystery as the events on the original road. The book is intended to help the reader be open to wider horizons and not a limited program, merely as the beginning of a new journey with the One who is the beginning and the end, the Alpha and the Omega.

---

[3] One of the various correspondence courses offered by the Catholic Home Study Institute of Leesburg, Virginia, for college credit or on a non-credit basis.

Appendix

Reflecting on the
Emmaus Principles

The Emmaus Principles
for the Teacher

1. The teacher knows who he or she is.

2. The teacher knows his or her mission.

3. The teacher approaches the students personally.

4. The teacher walks along with the students.

5. The teacher finds out where the students are.

6. The teacher explains from the perspective of the students.

7. The teacher invites the students to make a response.

8. The teacher leads the students to liturgy.

9. The students discuss the message among themselves.

10. The students go out to share the message.

Dates _____ _____ _____

1. Jesus knew who he was.

Reflections:

1. Jesus knew who he was.

More Reflections:

Dates _____   _____   _____

2. Jesus knew his mission.

Reflections:

2. Jesus knew his mission.

More Reflections:

Dates _____   _____   _____

**3. Jesus approached the
disciples in person.**

Reflections:

3. Jesus approached the disciples in person.

More Reflections:

Dates _____   _____   _____

4. Jesus walked along with them.

Reflections:

4. Jesus walked along with them.

More Reflections:

Dates _____   _____   _____

5. Jesus asked them a question.

Reflections:

5. Jesus asked them a question.

More Reflections:

Dates _____   _____   _____

6. Jesus said to them, "O foolish [dear witless] ones!"

Reflections:

6. Jesus said to them, "O foolish [dear witless] ones!"

More Reflections:

Dates _____   _____   _____

7. Jesus made as if to go further.

Reflections:

7. Jesus made as if to go further.

More Reflections:

Dates _____ _____ _____

**8. Jesus took bread, blessed it,
broke it, and distributed it...**

Reflections:

8. Jesus took bread, blessed it, broke it, and distributed it...

More Reflections:

Dates _____   _____   _____

9. They spoke with each other.

Reflections:

9. They spoke with each other.

___

More Reflections:

Dates _____ _____ _____

10. They got up immediately and returned to Jerusalem.

Reflections:

10. They got up immediately and returned to Jerusalem.

More Reflections:

Bibliography

Adam, Adolf. *The Liturgical Year: Its History and Its Meaning After the Reform of the Liturgy.* Translated by Matthew J. O'Connell. New York: Pueblo Publishing Company, 1981.

Alfonso, Sister Regina M. *How Jesus Taught: The Methods and Techniques of the Master.* New York: Alba House, 1986.

Aliaga Girbés, Emilio. *Teología del Tiempo Litúrgico.* Valencia: Facultad de Teología San Vicente Ferrer, Sección Diócesis, 1980.

Ashkar, Chor-Bishop Dominic. "Cyril of Jerusalem: His Catechesis on the Mysteries of Initiation and Our Own Catechesis." Paper prepared for Study of Catechetics, a graduate course at The Catholic University of America, 1988.

Assemblées du Seigneur. *Temps des dimanches verts.* Proclamer le Royaume de Dieu, no. 15. Bruges: Biblica, 1965.

Bandas, Rev. Rudolph G[eorge]. *Catechetics in the New Testament.* Milwaukee: The Bruce Publishing Company, 1935.

Barclay, William. *Fishers of Men*. Philadelphia: The Westminster Press, 1966.

———. *God's Young Church*. Philadelphia: The Westminster Press, 1970.

Baus, Karl, and Hubert Jedin. *From the Apostolic Community to Constantine*. New York: Herder and Herder, 1965.

Baus, Karl, et al. *The Imperial Church from Constantine to the Early Middle Ages*. Translated by Anselm Biggs. New York: The Seabury Press, 1980.

Beggiani, Msgr. Seely J. *Early Syriac Theology*. Lanham, Maryland: University Press of America, 1983.

———. *Introduction to the Eastern Christian Spirituality: the Syriac Tradition*. Scranton, Pennsylvania: University of Scranton Press, 1991.

Belisle, Augustin. *The Wheel of Becoming*. Petersham, Massachusetts: St. Bede's Publications, 1987.

Bennion, Lowell L[indsay]. *Jesus the Master Teacher*. Salt Lake City: Deseret Book Company, 1980.

Bergamini, Augusto. *Cristo Festa della Chiesa: Storia-teología-spiritualità-pastorale dell'Anno Liturgico*. Rome: Edizioni Paoline, 1982.

Bergling, Kurt. *Moral Development: The Validity of Kohlberg's Theory*. Stockholm: Almqvist & Wiskell International, 1981.

Blumberg, Sherry H., and Eugene B. Borowitz. "Religious Pluralism: a Jewish Perspective." In *Religious Pluralism and Religious Education*, edited by Norma H. Thompson. Birmingham, Alabama: Religious Education Press, n.d.

Breitigam, R. R. *The Teacher Sent from God*. Mountain View, California: Pacific Press Publishing Association, 1960.

Briggs Myers, Isabel. *Gifts Differing*. Palo Alto, California: Consulting Psychologists Press, 1980.

Bruner, Jerome S. *Toward a Theory of Instruction*. New York: W. W. Norton & Company, Inc., 1966.

Bryce, Mary Charles. "The Uniform Catechism Before and After Baltimore III." *The Living Light* 21, no. 1 (October 1984): 7-28.

Buisson, H[enri], S.J. "Le Christ et les disciples d'Emmaüs." *Catéchistes* 69 (janvier 1967), 67-72.

Burghardt, W. J., S.J. "Catechetics in the Early Church: Program and Psychology." *The Living Light* 1, no. 3 (Autumn 1964): 100-118.

Campbell, Anna S. "Toward a Systematic Catechesis: an Interpretation of *Catechesi Tradendae*." *The Living Light* 17, no. 4 (Winter 1980): 311-320.

Cary, Otis. *The First Christian School: The Teacher and the Pupils*. Boston: The Pilgrim Press, 1922.

Civardi, Luigi. *Gesù Educatore*. Turin: Società Editrice Internazionale, 1961.

Clark, Aubert, Rev., O.F.M. Conv. "Medieval Catechetics and the First Catechisms." *The Living Light* 1, no. 4 (Winter 1964): 92-107.

Colomb, Joseph, P.S.S. "The Catechetical Method of Saint Sulpice." In *Shaping the Christian Message*, edited by Gerard Sloyan. New York: Macmillan Company, 1958.

Corbon, Jean. *The Wellspring of Worship*. Translated by Matthew J. O'Connell. New York: Paulist Press, 1988.

Coriden, James A. "The Teaching Ministry of the Church—A Commentary." *The Living Light* 20, no. 2 (January 1984): 119-145.

Cranford, Clarence W[illiam]. *Taught by the Master*. Nashville: Broadman Press, 1956.

Crichton, J. D. "Religious Education in England in the Penal Days." In *Shaping the Christian Message: Essays in Religious Education*, edited by Gerard S. Sloyan. New York: The Macmillan Company, 1958.

Davies, J[ohn] G[ordon]. *The Early Christian Church*. New York: Holt, Rinehart and Winston, 1965.

Dewey, John. *The Sources of a Science of Education*. New York: H. Livewright, 1929.

Donin, Rabbi Hayim Halevy. *To Be a Jew: A Guide to Jewish Observance in Contemporary Life*. New York: Basic Books, Inc., Publishers, 1972.

―――. *To Raise a Jewish Child: A Guide for Parents*. New York: Basic Books, Inc., Publishers, 1977.

Doohan, Leonard. *Luke: The Perennial Spirituality*. Santa Fe, New Mexico: Bear & Company, 1985. Write to Resource Publications, Inc., 160 E. Virginia Street #290, San Jose, CA 95112-5876.

Downs, Thomas. *The Parish as Learning Community*. New York: Paulist Press, 1979.

Driggs, Howard R[oscoe]. *The Master's Art: An Activity Course in Gospel Teaching*. Independence, Missouri: Zion's Printing & Publishing Co., 1946.

Dubay, Thomas, S.M. *Pilgrims Pray*. New York: Alba House, 1974.

Edel, William W. *The Walk to Emmaus*. An Easter play. Nashville: Abingdon, 1980.

Eisner, Elliot W. *The Educational Imagination: On the Design and Evaluation of School Programs*. 2nd ed. New York: Macmillan Publishing Company, 1985.

Elias, John L. *The Foundations and Practice of Adult Religious Education*. Malabar, Florida: Robert E. Krieger Publishing Company, 1982.

Ellis, Samuel R. *Jesus, the Great Teacher*. Boston: The Christopher Publishing House, 1935.

Erikson, Erik. *Childhood and Society*. Rev. ed. New York: W. W. Norton, 1963.

―――. *Insight and Responsibility*. New York: W. W. Norton, 1964.

"Evangelizing in the Culture and Society of the United States and the Bishop as the Teacher of the Faith." *Meeting of His Holiness John Paul II with the Archbishops of the United States, March 8-11.* Washington, D.C.: United States Catholic Conference, 1989.

Filthaut, Theodor, ed. *Israel in Christian Religious Instruction.* South Bend, Indiana: University of Notre Dame Press, 1965.

Fitzmyer, Joseph A., S.J. Introduction to "The Gospel According to Luke (X-XXIV)." *The Bible.* Garden City, New York: Doubleday & Company, Inc., 1985.

Flannery, Austin, O.P. *Vatican Council II: The Conciliar and Post-Conciliar Documents.* Collegeville, Minnesota: The Liturgical Press, 1984.

Fowler, J[ames]. *Stages of Faith.* New York: Harper & Row, 1981.

Franklin, R. W., and Robert L. Spaeth. *Virgil Michel: American Catholic.* Collegeville, Minnesota: The Liturgical Press, 1988.

Freire, Paulo. *Pedagogy of the Oppressed.* New York: Herder and Herder, 1972.

Fuchs, Michael Adrian. "The Task of the Religious Educator in Religious Symbol Discovery." Ph.D. diss., Columbia University Teacher's College, 1979.

Furth, Hans G. *Piaget and Knowledge: Theoretical Foundations.* Englewood Cliffs, New Jersey: Prentice-Hall, Inc., 1969.

Gaffney, Sister M. Honor, O.P. "Development of the Liturgical Approach in Teaching Religion in the Elementary School." M.A. diss., Catholic University of America, 1955.

General Catechetical Directory (Directorium Catechisticum Generale). In *Teaching the Catholic Faith Today* by Msgr. Eugene Kevane. Boston: St. Paul Editions, 1982.

Genung, John F. *What a Carpenter Did with His Bible.* New York: Thomas Y. Crowell & Company, 1898.

Gillièron, Bernard. *Le Repas d'Emmaüs: Quand les yeux s'ouvrent sur le Christ ressuscité.* Aubonne: Editions du Moulin, 1984.

Gleeson, Thomas F., S.J. "History and Present Scene in Religious Education." *Teaching All Nations* 11, no. 2 (1974): 66-84.

Goldman, Ronald. *Religious Thinking from Childhood to Adolescence.* London: Routledge and Kegan Paul, 1964.

Gordon, Wm. J. J. *Synectics: the Development of Creative Capacity.* New York: Harper & Row, Publishers, 1961.

Grassi, Joseph A. *Teaching the Way: Jesus, the Early Church and Today.* Washington, D.C.: University Press of America, 1982.

Gray, R., and David Moberg. *The Church and the Older Person.* Nashville: Eerdmans, 1977.

Groome, Thomas H. "A Task of Present Dialectical Hermeneutics." *The Living Light* 14, no. 3 (Autumn 1977): 408-423.

Guild, Pat Burke, and Stephen Garger. *Marching to Different Drummers.* Alexandria, Virginia: Association for Supervision and Curriculum Development, 1985.

Guitton, Jean. "Les Disciples d'Emmaüs." In *Le Clair et l'Obscur.* Paris: Aubier-Montaigne, 1964.

Hagberg, Janet, and Richard Leider. *The Inventurers: Excursions in Life and Career Renewal.* Rev. ed. Reading, Massachusetts: Addison-Wesley Publishing Company, 1978.

Hald, Henry. "The Liturgical Element in Religious Instruction." *National Catholic Education Association Bulletin* 27 (1930): 493-502.

Hall, Jeremy. "The American Worship Movement: The Early Years." *Worship* 50 (1976): 472-489.

Hater, Robert J. "The Relationship Between Evangelization and Catechesis." A clarification/study paper commissioned by the National Conference of Diocesan Directors of Religious Education. Washington, D.C.: NCCD, 1981.

———. "Religious Education and Catechesis: a Shift in Focus." A clarification/study paper commissioned by the National Conference of Diocesan Directors of Religious Education. Washington, D.C.: NCCD, 1981.

———. "The Role of a Diocesan Religious Education Catechetical Office." A clarification/study paper commissioned by the National Conference of Diocesan Directors of Religious Education. Washington, D.C.: NCCD, 1982.

Heagle, John. *Our Journey Toward God*. Chicago: The Thomas More Press, 1977.

Hinnebusch, Paul, O.P. *Religious Life: A Living Liturgy*. New York: Sheed and Ward, 1965.

Horne, Herman Harrell. *Jesus the Master Teacher*. Grand Rapids, Michigan: Kregel Publications, 1964.

Hott, Rev. Geo. P. *Christ the Teacher*. Dayton, Ohio: U. B. Publishing House, 1900.

Hummel, Sister Marie Louis, A.M. "The Principle of Apperception in the Teaching of Christ." Ph.D. diss., The Catholic University of America, 1924.

Institute of Missionary Catechesis of the Pontifical Urban University, ed. *Going, TEACH...: Commentary on the Apostolic Exhortation "Catechesi Tradendae" of John Paul II*. Boston: St. Paul Editions, 1980.

Irwin, Kevin W. *Liturgical Theology: a Primer*. American Essays in Liturgy Series, edited by Edward Foley. Collegeville, Minnesota: The Liturgical Press, 1990.

Jackson, Pamela. "Cyril of Jerusalem's Use of Scripture in Catechesis." *Theological Studies* 52 (1991): 431-450.

Jacobs, Louis. *The Book of Jewish Belief*. New York: Behrman House, Inc., 1984.

Jeanne d'Arc, Soeur. *Les Pélerins d'Emmaüs*. Paris: Les Editions du Cerf, 1977.

John Paul II. "Mother of the Redeemer" ("Redemptoris Mater"). Encyclical letter. Boston: Daughters of St. Paul, 1987.

John Paul II, Catechist: The Text with Commentary and Discussion Questions of "Catechesi Tradendae," the Pope's New Charter for Religious Education Today. Chicago: Franciscan Herald Press, 1980.

Jones, Claude C. *The Teaching Methods of the Master.* St. Louis: The Bethany Press, 1957.

Jorgensen, Susan S. *Rekindling the Passion: Liturgical Renewal in Your Community.* San Jose, California: Resource Publications, Inc., 1993.

Jungmann, Josef, S.J. "Religious Education in Late Medieval Times." In *Shaping the Christian Message: Essays in Religious Education,* edited by Gerard S. Sloyan. New York: The Macmillan Company, 1958.

Kelly, Rev. Francis D. "A Catechetical Journey: Toward a Common Vision." *America* 159 (October 8, 1988): 222-227+.

Kemp, Raymond B. *A Journey in Faith: An Experience of the Catechumenate.* New York: Sadlier, 1979.

Kennedy, William Bean. "Christian Education Through History." In *An Introduction to Christian Education,* edited by Marvin J. Taylor. Nashville: Abingdon Press, 1966.

Kevane, Eugene. *Augustine the Educator: A Study in the Fundamentals of Christian Formation.* Westminster, Maryland: The Newman Press, 1964.

Kevane, Eugene, ed. *Creed and Catechetics: a Catechetical Commentary on the Creed of the People of God.* Boston: Daughters of St. Paul, 1978.

Kevane, Msgr. Eugene. Introduction (historical overview) to *Teaching the Catholic Faith Today: Twentieth Century Catechetical Documents of the Holy See.* Boston: St. Paul Editions, 1982.

Khouj, Abdullah Muhammed. "Education in Islam." In *Religious Pluralism and Religious Education*, edited by Norma H. Thompson. Birmingham, Alabama: Religious Education Press, 1988.

Kirby, Patricia. *Cognitive Style, Learning Style, and Transfer Skill Acquisition.* Information Series, no. 195. Columbus, Ohio: National Center for Research in Vocational Education, 1979.

Klein, Isaac. *A Guide to Jewish Religious Practice.* New York: The Jewish Theological Seminary of America, 1979.

Knowles, Malcolm. *The Adult Learner: A Neglected Species.* 4th ed. Houston: Gulf Publishing Company, 1990.

Koberg, Don, and Jim Bagnall. *The All-New Universal Traveler: a Soft-Systems Guide to Creativity, Problem-Solving, and the Process of Reaching Goals.* Los Altos, California: William Kaufmann, Inc., 1981.

Kohlberg, Lawrence. "Revisions in the Theory and Practice of Moral Development." *New Directions for Child Development* 2 (1978): 83-88.

Kohlberg, Lawrence, and E. Turiel. *Recent Research in Moral Judgment.* New York: Holt, Rinehart and Winston, Inc., 1971.

L'anno Liturgico. Atti della XI Settimana di studio dell'Associazione Professori di Liturgia, Brescia, 23-27 agosto 1982. Casale Monferrato: Casa Editrice Marietti, 1983.

LaHaye, Tim. *Transformed Temperaments.* Wheaton, Illinois: Tyndale House Publishers, 1973.

Leonard, George Burr. *Education and Ecstasy.* New York: Delacorte Press, 1968.

Lever, Katherine. *The Perfect Teacher.* New York: The Seabury Press, 1964.

Levinson, D., and Associates. *The Seasons of a Man's Life.* New York: Knopf, 1978.

Lombaerts, Herman. "Religious Education Today and the Catechism." *Word in Life* 34, no. 1 (February 1986): 13-19.

Losoncy, Lawrence. *Religious Education and the Life Cycle.* Bethlehem, Pennsylvania: Catechetical Communications, 1977.

Lozanov, Georgi. *Suggestology and Outlines of Suggestopedy.* New York: Gordon and Breach, 1978.

Marcia, J. "Ego Identity Status: Relationship to Self-Esteem, General Maladjustment, and Authoritarianism." *Journal of Personality* 35 (1967): 118-133.

Marquis, John A. *Learning to Teach from the Master Teacher.* Philadelphia: The Westminster Press, 1913.

Marthaler, Berard L. "Socialization as a Model for Catechetics." In *Foundations of Religious Education,* edited by Padraic O'Hare. New York: Paulist Press, 1975.

Mathews, H. F. *Revolution in Religious Education: A Commentary.* Wallington, Surrey, England: The Religious Education Press, Ltd., 1966.

Maves, Paul. "Religious Development in Adulthood." In *Research on Religious Development: a Comprehensive Handbook,* edited by M. Strommen. A project of the Religious Education Association. New York: Hawthorn, 1971.

Mayer, Frederick. *Education for Creative Living.* New York: Whittier Books, Inc., 1959.

McAlpine, Stuart. *The Road Best Traveled.* Nashville: Thomas Nelson Publishers, 1991.

McCarthy, Bernice. *The 4MAT System: Teaching to Learning Styles with Right/Left Mode Techniques.* Barrington, Illinois: Excel, Inc., 1987.

McKoy, Charles Francis. *The Art of Jesus as a Teacher.* Philadelphia: The Judson Press, 1930.

Megivern, James J., ed. *Worship & Liturgy.* Official Catholic Teachings Series. Wilmington, North Carolina: A Consortium Book, 1978.

Meier, David. "New Age Learning: From Linear to Geodesic." *Training and Development Journal* 39, no. 5 (May 1985): 40-43.

Milgram, Roberta Mades. "A Study of the Inquiry-Discovery Method in Teaching Moral Concepts." Ph.D. diss., The American University, 1969.

Michel, Virgil, O.S.B. "Rediscovering the Obvious: Liturgy and the Psychology of Education." *Orate Fratres* 14 (October 27, 1940): 529-532.

Moran, Gabriel. *Catechesis of Revelation.* New York: Herder and Herder, 1966.

Moule, Right Rev. H[andley] C[arr] G[lyn]. *Emmaus.* London: Samuel Bagster & Sons Limited, 1912.

Murray, Robert. *Symbols of Church and Kingdom: a Study in Early Syriac Tradition.* London: Cambridge University Press, 1975.

National Association of Secondary School Principals. *Student Learning Styles and Brain Behavior: Programs, Instrumentation, Research.* Reston, Virginia: NASSP, 1982.

Neville, Gwen Kennedy, and John H. Westerhoff, III. *Learning Through Liturgy.* New York: The Seabury Press, 1978.

O'Malley, William J., S.J. "Toward an Adult Spirituality." *America* 161 (November 18, 1989): 341-344.

Paulin, A. *St. Cyrille de Jérusalem Catéchète.* Paris: Les Editions du Cerf, 1959.

Piaget, Jean. *The Origins of Intelligence in Children.* New York: International Universities Press, 1952.

Piper, David R. *How Would Jesus Teach?* Elgin, Illinois: David C. Cook Publishing Company, 1931.

Powers, John. *Eucharistic Theology.* New York: Herder and Herder, 1967.

Rahner, Karl. *The Eternal Year.* Translated by John Shea, S.S. Baltimore: Helicon Press, Inc., 1964.

Rahner, Karl, ed. *Sacramentum Mundi: an Encyclopedia of Theology.* New York: Herder and Herder, 1968-70.

Ramirez, Manuel, III, and Alfredo Castañeda. *Cultural Democracy, Bicognitive Development, and Education.* New York: Academic Press, 1974.

Rixon, Lilas D. *How Jesus Taught: Methods and Roles of Jesus Christ the Teacher.* Croydon, New South Wales, Australia: Sydney Missionary and Bible College, 1977.

Rochelle, Jay C. *The Revolutionary Year: Recapturing the Meaning of the Christian Year.* Philadelphia: Fortress Press, 1973.

Rogers, Carl R. *Freedom to Learn.* Columbus, Ohio: Charles E. Merrill, 1969.

Roldán, Alexander. *Personality Types and Holiness.* Translated by Gregory McCaskey. Staten Island, New York: Alba House, 1968.

Russell, William H[enry]. *Jesus the Divine Teacher.* New York: P. J. Kenedy & Sons, 1944.

Schanz, Rev. John P. *The Sacraments of Life and Worship.* Milwaukee: The Bruce Publishing Company, 1966.

Schroeder, Ruth Jones, and Irene Swanson Slaght. *New Testament Studies in Principles of Teaching and Principles of Worship.* Prepared from "Principles of Teaching as Revealed by the Teaching Ministry of Jesus" and "Principles and Practice of Worship as Disclosed in the Four Gospels," Master's theses, Eastern Baptist Theological Seminary, June 1939.

Scott, A. Kieran. "Catechesis and Religious Education: Uncovering the Nature of Our Work." *PACE (Professional Approaches in Christian Education)* 12. Winona, Minnesota: Saint Mary's Press, 1981-82.

———. "Revelation: The Search for a Common Starting Point." *PACE (Professional Approaches in Christian Education)* 12. Winona, Minnesota: Saint Mary's Press, 1981-82.

Sharing the Light of Faith: National Catechetical Directory for Catholics of the United States. Washington, D.C.: United States Catholic Conference, 1979.

Skinner, B. F. *Walden II.* New York: Macmillan Publishing Company, 1976.

————. *Contingencies of Reinforcement.* Englewood Cliffs, New Jersey: Prentice-Hall, Inc., 1969.

Sloyan, Gerard S., ed. *Shaping the Christian Message: Essays in Religious Education.* New York: The Macmillan Company, 1958.

Strassfeld, Michael, Betsy Platkin Teutsch, and Arnold M. Eisen. *The Jewish Holidays: A Guide and Commentary.* New York: Harper & Row, Publishers, 1985.

Swete, Henry Barclay. *Studies in the Teaching of Our Lord.* 2nd ed. London: Hodder and Stoughton, 1904.

Talayero, José. *El Método de Enseñanza de Jesucristo.* Saragossa: Heraldo de Aragón, 1951.

Teaching the Catholic Faith Today: Twentieth Century Catechetical Documents of the Holy See. Boston: St. Paul Editions, 1982.

Thomson, Bishop E[dward] A. *Christ as a Teacher.* New York: Phillips & Hunt, 1883.

Ulich, Robert. *A History of Religious Education: Documents and Interpretation from the Judaeo-Christian Tradition.* New York: New York University Press, 1968.

Warren, Michael, ed. *Sourcebook for Modern Catechetics.* Winona, Minnesota: Saint Mary's Press, 1983.

Westerhoff, John H., III. *A Pilgrim People: Learning Through the Church Year.* New York: The Seabury Press, 1984.

————. "Understanding the Problem of Faithfulness" and "The Future: Framing an Alternative for the Future of Catechesis." In *A Faithful Church: Issues in the History of Catechesis,* edited by John H. Westerhoff, III, and O. C. Edwards, Jr. Wilton, Connecticut: Morehouse-Barlow Co., Inc., 1981.

Westerhoff, John H., III, and O. C. Edwards, Jr., eds. *A Faithful Church: Issues in the History of Catechesis*. Wilton, Connecticut: Morehouse-Barlow Co., Inc., 1981.

Wouk, Herman. *This Is My God: The Jewish Way of Life*. Boston: Little, Brown and Co., 1988.

Wuerl, Bishop Donald W., Ronald Lawler, O.F.M. Cap., and Thomas Comerford Lawler, eds. *The Teaching of Christ: a Catholic Catechism for Adults*. 3rd ed. Huntington, Indiana: Our Sunday Visitor Publishing Division, 1991.

Zadra, Dario. *Il Tempo Simbolico: la Liturgia della Vita*. Brescia: Editrice Morcelliana S.p.A., 1985.

CELEBRATING THE LECTIONARY
Changes Peoples Lives!

CELEBRATING THE LECTIONARY (CTL) is a curriculum for catechesis and Children's Liturgy of the Word. CTL is social-justice oriented to help you keep connected with world issues. All you need is a volunteer, a lectionary or Bible, and a teaching packet for each class. Teaching packets include background sheets, lesson pans, and student handouts.

Celebrating
The Lectionary

1993-94
A Grassroots Curriculum
for Roman Catholic
Catechesis and Celebration

Order a free 48-page information booklet by calling 1-800-736-7600 or by checking the box on the order form on the next page. The free booklet contains:

- An overview of the year, including the themes for each unit.

- A sample of a unit outline covering the readings, themes and purpose for each lesson.

- Complete sample lessons for **all age groups** for one Sunday's readings (October 10, 1993).

- Samples of the Children's Liturgy of the Word (CLOW) and Family Handout master (English and Spanish).

- How to get a more detailed preview packet.

- How to order and use CTL packets.

Stories for Religious Education

TELLING STORIES LIKE JESUS DID
Creative Parables for Teachers
Christelle L. Estrada

Paper, $8.95, 98 pages, 5½" x 8½"
ISBN 0-89390-097-4

Bring home the heart of Jesus' message to your students by personalizing the parables of Luke. Each chapter includes introductory comments and questions, an easy-to-use storyline, and discussion questions for primary, secondary, and junior high grades.

PARABLES FOR LITTLE PEOPLE

Paper, $7.95, 101 pages, 5½" x 8½"
ISBN 0-89390-034-6

MORE PARABLES FOR LITTLE PEOPLE

both by Lawrence Castagnola, SJ

Paper, $8.95, 82 pages, 5½" x 8½"
ISBN 0-89390-095-8

With the stories in these companion volumes, Castagnola helps you reach young listeners through teaching, preaching, or the simple pleasures of storytelling. Both contain stories with Gospel themes such as sharing, caring, non-violence, and women's rights.

STORIES FOR CHRISTIAN INITIATION
Joseph J. Juknialis

Paper, $8.95, 152 pages, 6" x 9"
ISBN 0-89390-205-5

These imaginative stories resonate with key lectionary passages and stages of the catechumenate — from pre-catechumenate to mystagogia. Great for starting discussions, the reflections, questions, and rituals will help catechumens tell their own stories.

STORIES TO INVITE FAITH-SHARING
Experiencing the Lord through the Seasons
Mary McEntee McGill

Paperbound, $8.95, 128 pages, 5½" x 8½"
ISBN 0-89390-230-6

The author tells twenty stories based on real-life experiences, which in turn can help readers recognize God's presence in their everyday life. Each story includes reflections and questions to help start the discussion process. Great for faith-sharing groups, workshops, and retreats.

Order Form

Order these resources from your local bookstore, or complete and mail or fax this form to:

☐ Please send me a **FREE** CELEBRATING THE LECTIONARY information booklet.

☐ Please enter my order for the following books:

QTY	TITLE	PRICE	TOTAL

Subtotal: _____

CA residents add 7¼% sales tax
(Santa Clara Co. residents, 8¼%): _____

Postage and handling
($2 for order up to $20; 10% of order over $20 but less than $150; $15 for order of $150 or more): _____

Total: _____

Resource Publications, Inc.
160 E. Virginia Street #290-A7
San Jose, CA 95112-5876
(408) 286-8505
(408) 287-8748 FAX

☐ My check or money order is enclosed.

☐ Charge my ☐ VISA ☐ MC.

Expiration Date _____

Card # _____ - _____ - _____ - _____

Signature _____

Name (print) _____

Institution _____

Street _____

City/State/ZIP _____

Thank you for your order!